To Paula

Keep On
Showing Up...
Listening....
&
Caring...

Marcus Alsh
2017

I Have a Story to Tell

MARSIALLE ARBUCKLE

authorHOUSE®

AuthorHouse™
1663 Liberty Drive
Bloomington, IN 47403
www.authorhouse.com
Phone: 1-800-839-8640

First published by AuthorHouse 6/16/2010

ISBN: 978-1-4520-1269-8 (e)
ISBN: 978-1-4520-1270-4 (sc)
ISBN: 978-1-4520-1271-1 (hc)

Library of Congress Control Number: 2010905831

Printed in the United States of America
Bloomington, Indiana

This book is printed on acid-free paper.

Scripture quotations noted are from
 The King James Version of the Holy Bible.
Copyright 1987 by Thomas Nelson, Inc.

Design and layout of this book were done by Author House Publishing Company

Table of Contents

Preface

Marsialle Arbuckle has had a life full of tragedy and triumph, pain and glory, sorrow and celebration. Throughout this work Marsialle chronicles various events of his life and the impact those events have had on him, his family, his relationships and the world around him.

As the reader is led through the twists and turns that life can create, the reader will be emotionally moved by the vivid descriptions of traumatic episodes that are life and death battles for survival.

The book is intended to stimulate the mind and provoke discussion with the review of various aspects of Marsialle's life. The book will inform and motivate those that are part of the Foster Care System, or from a dysfunctional family and dealing with the ravages of substance abuse. The book will inspire and uplift individuals and families that are battling heart disease, cancer, vascular disease or some other catastrophic health issue. This book demonstrates the awesome power of love, understanding, and prayer.

The creation of this book, "I Have A Story To Tell" has resulted in the establishment of "The Center for Urban Youth & Family Development." The Center currently operates three program elements which include Youth Workforce and Life Skills Development and Substance Abuse Prevention, Health Management, and Community Activism.

In our work with youth in Foster Care our vision is to integrate group discussions with academic and skills development, i.e. Tutoring, the creation of a "Five Year Life Plan," and Mentoring. We believe those elements along with an introduction to various cultural experiences to develop alternative interests, combined will influence and impact various decisions and actions on an individual, family, and community level; for positive change.

We would love to hear from you. Your comments, suggestions and recommendations are requested and will be sincerely appreciated. Contact us at: www.THECENTERFORURBANYOUTHANDFAMILYDEVELOPMENT.ORG

Dedication

This book is dedicated to the memory of Rosie & Walter Yearby my foster parents. I also dedicate it to the children and families, social workers and staff that are a part of the Foster Care System. My life is an example of what all of the well meaning individuals intended to be the result and output of the system that they designed. I pray that your lives be blessed to yield even better results and a greater output.

I also dedicate this book to the University of Michigan Survival Flight team. You risk your lives to save the lives of others, and one of those other lives was mine. I hope that the result of your actions with regard to me will make you all joyful and proud that you did what did and you do what you do.

Finally I dedicate this book to any individual or family that is facing a catastrophic health issue. Reading this book should bring you hope. The hope to believe in things that you cannot fully understand or control. Know that there is a power greater than man and that power goes beyond our understanding.

Acknowledgments

I first must thank God, without his love I would be nothing.

Thank you to my brothers Michael, Montclair, Robert, and my sister Mercedes, for letting me tell my story; because my story is your story. I hope our story can help someone.

Thank you to my brothers Kevin, Kenny, and Robert for being loving in-laws rather than out-laws...the same to you my loving sisters Beverly and Andrea.

Thank you to my brothers of Omega, it's so good to be a "Son of Blood & Thunder." You've shared with me the characteristics of manhood, and helped me to learn the value of scholarship, you instilled through example perseverance, and revealed to me that with those three traits one is not only in the position to, but obligated to provide uplift. When I die bury me deep; and bury at my feet; those pearls of Omega!

Thank you to my lodge brothers of the "Grand Ole Order" and to my sisters of the Household, how good and pleasant it is to share your friendship, love, and to know the truth as you all do, for together those three elements of life lead us to peace, happiness, and prosperity.

Thank you to Ms. Estelle Chapman, I penned this novel in your ninety-eight year of life. We kept our promise to each other that you would get and opportunity to enjoy it. Your life is an example of what God can do as is mine. You are an inspiration to us all.

Thank you to Mrs. Shenae Pruitt and Mr. Eugene Gillis, the established authors in the family. Both your works inspired me to move forward and not stop until the job was done.

Thank you to my son Theodore, you have and continue to live up to all of our expectations and on most occasions you exceed them.

Thank you to all my "grands"...Rodney, Noah, and Jonah. You guys are the greatest, really you are, really. I had to finish this project to leave you evidence that whatever you set your mind to doing; you can accomplish it, just conceive it, believe it, and then achieve it, CBA or ABC backwards.

Finally I give thanks and my everlasting gratitude to my wife Barbara (I love you with a passion that is uncontested) and my children Jamillah (my Editor, thank you so much) and Marseille, Jr. (I'm so proud of you).

Introduction

I have a story to tell. The story has taken fifty years to unfold, and new twists seem to be on the horizon. I've told different bits and pieces of the story to various people over time. In each instance the response is always the same, "You should write a book and tell the entire story." I believe that is because each element, section, bit and piece of the story reflects triumph over tragedy and the greatness of God, His goodness and mercy, and most importantly the trueness of the Holy Word. My story seems to be one that is uplifting and a blessing to those that I share it with, and I'd like for it to be available as a resource to everyone. So, here it is.

In 1958, the U.S. Department of Family and Children deems the orphanage system a failure and not capable of meeting the growing needs of children across the nation. Many of the children were not truly orphans and were only in temporary need of assistance. They concluded that the rearing of children should be conducted in a family atmosphere where nurturing and development take place naturally, unlike the cold and impersonal environments that an institution like the orphanage` system had developed into. There also needed to be a method for addressing the needs of children that would be in the system short term as well as long term.

The new system, called the Foster Parent Program, would replace orphanages. This system would integrate children into families and homes that were already established. Families would be screened for fitness, and trained to deal with the special needs of children that are displaced from their biological parents. A federal model was created, but each state was required to establish and develop a Foster Child Care Program. The state of Indiana took on the challenge and launched a Foster Child Care Program. This program serves as the link between the characters involved in this story. To understand their backgrounds will provide insight on their behavior and how that behavior has impacted me over the years. We'll start with Willie Arbuckle, Sr.

Chapter 1

Willie was the youngest of five siblings. There were three sisters Rose, Delilah, and Louise; along with one older brother, George. They were the first generation of Arbuckles to migrate from the South (Tennessee) to Chicago during WWII. The Arbuckles were the children of a minister and schoolteacher, so they were fairly well educated. Rose and Louise married and had children of their own. George went off to the war and returned to marry Lillian and had no children. After a short while in Chicago, Delilah and her brother Willie Sr. moved to Gary, Indiana. Willie Sr. secured employment as a welder at the United States Steel Company factory in Gary. He had a brief marriage, which ended in divorce. The marriage resulted in the birth of one son, Willie Arbuckle, Jr. my biological father.

Mr. Arbuckle provided a home for Willie, Jr. along with the assistance of the boy's aunt Delilah while maintaining the lifestyle of a bachelor. In the 1940's, employees of steel mills earned great wages for the economic period. Like the autoworkers of Michigan, steelworker wages afforded skilled workers to have upper-middleclass incomes. As single parents often do, Willie Sr. attempted to substitute personal attention and time with purchased items. As a teenager Willie Jr. was big and excelled at sports, in particular football. This fact combined with his economic means made Jr. very popular with the ladies. The true fancy of his eye was Augustine Reid, a classmate. Willie, Jr. received a football scholarship from a small school in St. Louis. He only completed one year and returned to Gary, IN. Willie, Jr. married his high school sweetheart Augustine; together they had three children, Montclair, Michael, and Marsialle. Augustine Arbuckle is my biological mother.

Chapter 2

Next is Walter Yearby, the youngest of three siblings. Walter had one older brother, James, and a younger sister, Carrie B. Walter had migrated to Chicago with his mother, brother and sister as a teenager from the South (Georgia). Walter had no formal schooling and could only write his name, however, he had learned to count money, and had a natural talent to operate and work with machinery. Both James and Carrie B. married and had children. Although Carrie B's marriage ended, she reared her children with a strong hand, her son Carl went on to become a Supreme Court Justice for the state of Illinois.

Walter earned money to support himself, his mother, sister and her kids as a mechanic. To make ends meet, in the evenings he would work as a carrier of ice blocks to high-rise apartments. That's where he met Rosie Steel, an extremely attractive woman that was a bit older and educated (15 years/ third grade). Walter enlisted in the war and was stationed in the Philippines. He was a part of a transportation company and functioned as a mechanic and truck driver. During action in the

South Pacific Theater, he committed an act of valor for which he was awarded the Bronze Star. Walter married Rosie Steel while home on leave and returned to war. After completing his enlistment term and being honorably discharged from service, Walter returned to Chicago to begin life with his new wife. After a short while Walter secured employment at Universal Atlas Cement Company, a division of U.S. Steel, located in the Indiana Harbor. A year later he and Rosie moved into a newly constructed home in Gary, Indiana. Walter and Rosie Yearby are my God appointed mother and father.

Walter and Rosie had settled into their new home. In the early 1950's, Gary, Indiana was blooming into a "bedroom" community of Chicago but was not quite there yet. Their two-bedroom cottage seemed to be in the middle of nowhere. The street was unpaved, and only three or four other homes where on the block. With Walter working long hours, 2240 Arthur Street had become a lonely place. Walter and Rosie knew that children would be the answer, but that was not to be. Due to "physical" issues, Rosie could not have children. The announcement of this new Foster Child Care Program was the answer. Rosie could qualify for the program and the child would cure the loneliness issue as well as position Rosie to become a contributing member to the household finances because foster parents are compensated.

Rosie's first assignment was David, a toddler placed in her care whose mother was negligent. David was returned to his natural mother after five or six months. The separation was very difficult for Rosie. Within a very short time period, Rosie was reassigned with Barbara Gene and her little brother Hildred. Barbara Gene was an adolescent girl and Hildred was

4

7 or 8. Barbara Gene had a bed wetting issue, and little Hildred was malnourished. Rosie helped Barbara Gene overcome her bed wetting via a questionable method, public humiliation. She would force Hildred to wash her soiled linens and pajamas on the front porch while being yelled at for the occurrence. The other kids in the neighborhood would hear the yelling and know why it was happening; the embarrassment must have been overwhelming. In today's society, such harsh methods would be viewed as abusive regardless of the effectiveness of the approach. However, Rosie prided herself on the fact that the approach did work and only required two such sessions. Rosie also took pride in the fact that she quickly "fattened up" Hildred by "<u>making him</u>" clean his plate, and feeding him garden grown fresh vegetables like collard greens, peas, potatoes, and sweet corn on the cob. Considering a 7- or 8-year-old's disdain for vegetables, I'm sure the "making him" part of the ordeal involved a belt, which Rosie did not believe in sparing. Despite her stern discipline, Rosie developed a very close relationship with the two. This was evidenced by random visits from one or both of the children over the years as they reached adulthood. Each visit would be filled with declarations of love and comments from the kids like, "You treated me better than my real parents ever did." Those two children also were reunited with their parents within a year. Rosie requested that her next placement be long-term because the separations were too difficult for her. She had an uncanny capability to establish and to maintain a bond with children in a very short period of time and the separations were emotionally draining for her.

Chapter 3

Willie Jr. returned to Gary, Indiana from a year of college a wild man. He was bigger and stronger than ever due to training table meals and weight room workouts. He had become even more street wise from hanging out with other "slick" guys from St. Louis and was ready to set the world on its edge. One thing slowed him, he was in love. So, as the times pretty much dictated, he married his high school sweetheart, Augustine, and they started making babies. While times have changed, certain scenarios haven't, young couple gets married and has a child. The mother is supposed to stay at home and care for the kid, he runs the street. This couple had a slight deviation, she ran the street with him and the baby is cared for by Auntie Delilah. While running the street, they develop a heroin addiction. To support their habit they start team shoplifting and commit other acts of larceny. Somehow in the midst of this activity they create another child. Delilah complains to her brother and sisters in Chicago that her nephew is out of control. As the aunts and uncle from Chicago hear of Willie

Jr.'s exploits they caution their brother to get involved in his son's life and "turn him around." Senior responds that Jr. is a grown man and must be both responsible and accountable for his actions. The children are his children and their quality of life is relative to what he can provide for them, not what their Grandfather or any of the rest of the family can provide. That disposition and those words would have a lasting impact on the lives of my siblings and me, as they would ultimately serve as the rationale and justification for a lack of family support at a critical time. Again in the midst of this turmoil Willie, Jr. and Augustine conceive a third child, me.

Life with parents that are heroin addicts is every bit as terrible as one can imagine. We moved from one dump to another. We suffered abuse from the parents as well as other addicts that frequented our place or, at the flop-house where we were as our parents got a fix or shot-up. My oldest brother recalls a lot of physical abuse. Even though he was only three or four years old, he recalls beatings that he suffered because he was not taking care of our brother Michael and or me. I don't recall very much about the two years that I lived in the care of Willie, Jr. and Augustine. I bear a scar on the instep of my right foot that is the result of a burn or scalding at the hands of Augustine. My only vivid memory is one of horror. My brothers and I were left alone in a room for a long period of time (turns out it was three days). Our food source was a pan of cornbread that was left in the middle of the floor. I was not capable of cleaning myself nor was I fully potty trained. By the early morning of day two I had waste crusted to my backside which irritated and burned. I began to cry so violently that my brothers carried me outdoors and attempted to lift me over a fence so a neighbor would see and help me. The idea worked, she pulled me over the fence, took me into her home and cleaned me. She also contacted our grandfather who got our parents to return home. Montclair and Michael suffered a beating as the reward for their heroic act.

The incident caused uproar from the family. Auntie Delilah had learned of the incident from our grandfather, her brother Willie, Sr., and informed the others in Chicago. She told them of the level of support that she was providing but made it clear that she, a single woman, could not and would not take in the three sons of her nephew, no matter how much she loved him or how cute the kids are. The family did as most families will do; they pointed the finger away from the Arbuckle family. They concluded that our mother Augustine was the real culprit, and not their family member our father Willie Jr. The Arbuckle clan cleared its' conscious by holding Augustine responsible and believing that she and her family should be the ones to manage the issue. They also reflected back on the words from Willie, Sr., "Jr. is a grown man and must be both responsible and accountable for his actions. The children are his children and their quality of life is relative to what he can provide for them, not what their Grandfather or any of the rest of the family can provide." That being said, the Arbuckle clan decided to "let the chips (my brothers and me) falls where they may."

News of the family discussion got back to Jr. and Augustine. They were told in no uncertain terms that not only were they not going to receive support but that the baby-sitting service of Auntie Delilah was also going to end. These children were their responsibility and they were going to have to manage it. I guess you could call it tough love. Willie, Jr. and Augustine concluded that they had to do something. They had to get rid of us so they could be free. The course of action that they followed is shocking. Even after having experienced it and survived, I find it almost impossible to believe that they chose to do as they did. To state it in a pleasant fashion, they analyzed the situation, researched possible alternatives and concluded that the Foster Child Care Program would be a viable solution for them. To state it in terms of reality, they had heard of the Foster Child Care Program and their vague understanding of it was that the authorities keep your kids for a while and then you can get them back. With the plan in place the next step was to execute.

After doing some checking in the streets, Willie, Jr. discovered that they couldn't just go and turn the kids in to the Foster Child Care Program folks. In fact the only way kids are in the program is if the state takes the kids from the parents for some reason. Little did he know that had the authorities been notified of their neglect a couple of months earlier, their issue would have been resolved. Willie, Jr. and Augustine had already had several run-ins with the Gary Police and concluded that the wrong type of abuse or neglect could lead to a police problem. Their heroin soaked minds decided that abandonment would not cause police problems. So, on a windy, gray, and chilly mid-October afternoon Willie and Augustine gathered us into the car and drove to 13th and Broadway in downtown Gary, Indiana. They parked across the street from the front entrance of the city courthouse and jail. The car was just a few feet beyond the stairwell that led down to the Chili Bowl Diner. This diner was below street level so the stairwell led down. They took us out of the car and walked us across the street to the steps that led up to the court house. They lined us up side by side and Augustine said, "I know you boys are hungry, so I want you to stand right here and don't move, your daddy and I'll go and get you something to eat." They walked away and never returned.

My memory of the event is foggy but my oldest brother Montclair recalls the incident with bone chilling clarity. He remembers watching as they went back across the street and down the stairwell into the diner. He remembers how one or the other would stand in the stairwell and peek out at us and then look at their watch as if to say how long before the Foster Child Care Program folks come out and get them. He remembers how they both came up the stairs of the diner and how Willie, Jr. got into the car and Augustine came back across to us and said, "They ain't got nothing good for y'all down there, so we're going to go someplace else, but y'all just wait right here and we'll be back." He remembers tears forming in her eyes as Willie, Jr. called out to her to hurry up and come on and how she said, "Now y'all be good and stay right here, cause we'll be back, I promise."

Chapter 4

My brother Montclair recalls how we stood in that spot for more than another two hours. Three little boys ages 2, 3, and 4 just standing there on the steps of the city courthouse, cars driving past on the street. People coming and going, passing us by and looking. Not at the three little boys standing there alone with no adult supervision. They were looking because our clothes were old, torn, and dirty. Montclair recalls how the evening sky began to approach and the courthouse employees all filed past us without a word. It seems as if we all recall the next event as if it happened just a day ago. Maybe we remember because it was a miracle that we were a part of.

A car pulled up in front of the courthouse and stopped almost directly in front of us. Within two or three minutes a woman scurried down the courthouse steps past us to get into the car, but she paused and gave us a glaring look. The car drove off, but they must have only circled the block because within two or three minutes the car was back. The lady got out and approached us; she spoke to Montclair, "What are you boys doing here?" Maybe it was the expression on his face or the tone of pain in his voice that alerted the lady, or her professional training, but somehow she knew our plight before Montclair could explain. She said, "Well my name is Mrs. Fletcher and I think you should come with my husband and me." She then gathered us together and walked down to the car. Michael began to cry and complain that we would be in trouble if we moved because, "Mommy and daddy are coming back to get us and they won't be able to find us if we're gone." I said nothing as I crawled into the backseat of the big sedan with Michael. Montclair got in the front seat between our rescuers.

Although we were too young to realize it at the time, God had intervened and a miracle had been performed. Think about it, of all the people that saw us that day, vehicles that passed us by, the person that noticed three little boys standing alone was not a pedophile or a child molester. It was not some individual that would have sold us into black market slavery or worse. The person happened to be a Social Worker and representative of the Foster Child Care Program.

Michael & I on our first day at the Yearby's – circa 1960

Chapter 5

Psalm 27:10, When my father and my mother forsake me, then the Lord will take me up. Although my upbringing from age two through eighteen involved countless hours in church, and we frequently read and studied the Bible, I did not know of that verse until seven or eight years ago. My familiarity with Psalm 27 was limited to **verse 1, The Lord is my light and my salvation; whom shall I fear? The Lord is the strength of my life; of whom shall I be afraid?** That verse had been and continues to be one of my favorite Bible verses because of the boldness of the speaker. He appears to view God as a defense that renders him undefeatable to the offensive of any foe. I could personally relate to feeling the awesome power of God as a defense and shield against all.

During a mid-month Sunday morning worship service the minister chose Psalm 27:1-3 as one of several scriptures for his sermon. Psalm was the last to be read. As the good reverend began to deliver the pre-sermon commentary, I casually read on as a preoccupation to the intense listening that a sermon deserves and receives from me. I briefly glanced at the entire 27th Psalm and noticed that it was rather short and would be a brief distraction and concluded that I would read it all. Midway through I had no idea of what a profound effect the tenth verse of this beautiful song of prayer, praise, and promise would have on me. This verse is a biblical promise to me personally; which had been kept and never broken. I had no way of knowing the impact that the fifteen words would have on my life at the time and in the future. As I read the verse the words seemed to jump off the page. Fifteen words which were so personal, and so internal to my situation. The evidence of the truth and the realness of the statement that I was reading, was being reflected in my very existence and being. Reading that verse seemed like a gigantic boost to my faith. How could I possibly have any fear of any one or thing for there it was in black and white I was truly a child of God. In the most real and literal sense of the fifteen words, I Marsialle DuShant Arbuckle was really one of God's children. No need for translation of Greek root words, no need for theological interpretation by a biblical scholar. No need for in-depth analysis of the context in which the words were spoken or the intent of the speaker. It said what it meant and it meant what it said; **When my father and my mother forsake me, then the Lord will take me up!** My father and mother had forsaken me and God had taken me up! What a glorious revelation, I was one of God's chosen ones because of a special reason. What honor, I was one of God's chosen ones because God had a plan for me. What power, I was one of God's chosen ones because God had turned a tragedy into a triumph. What responsibility, I'm one of God's chosen ones because God wants to use me for something.

God's saving grace had intervened in my life and began the history of miraculous events that provide proof of **II Corinthians 12:9, And he said unto me, My grace is sufficient for thee: for my strength is made perfect in weakness....** Three little boys, vulnerable to the entire would, but by His grace rescued and given an opportunity to live a life of peace, happiness, and prosperity. We were given an opportunity to live a life of power. The power of one of God's chosen ones. Once again providing proof of **II Corinthians 13:4, For though he was crucified through weakness, yet he liveth by the power of God. For we also are weak in him, but we shall live with him by the power of God towards you.**

Chapter 6

As I returned my attention to the Sunday services that day, I couldn't get the verse out of my mind. That evening I read the verse again and began to reflect. As I looked back over my life the events started to reflect a pattern. A pattern of miraculous situations and circumstances that had, and continue to occur. It was as if God himself had looked down and saw us standing there that October afternoon and said, "Oh no, three of my little ones are in trouble. And is that Marsialle, this can't happen, I have plans for him. He's to do some things thirty-five years from now that will impact the lives of thirty-five or forty young men who will then change the world years from then. Changes that could impact the lives of thousands." So God allowed His grace to save me by sending a Social Worker. Then God began His sustaining grace by identifying two of His most trusted servants to assign to my care. They were two of God's servants that would give me love and nurturing. God provided a new set of parents that would reveal Christianity to me and educate me. Parents that would sacrifice having items for themselves so I could take piano lessons and trumpet lessons. Parents that would give guidance and motivation to succeed and excel in a time that young African American men faced overwhelming obstacles like racism, discrimination, economic disparity, drugs, crime and violence.

As I continued to reflect on my life I began to see many things that I had taken for granted, were truly miracles. There were teachers and instructors that had gone the extra mile to help me. Statements that were made that were intended to insult and hurt me but instead had motivated me. One such incident occurred on the last day of my sixth grade experience at Banneker Elementary School in Gary, Indiana. As was tradition in the Gary Public School system, this would be our last day attending the elementary school. Next year we would move on to grammar or middle school as it was called. Our teacher was giving her final farewell address to her most treasured students, the accelerated students. This classroom of children had excelled on various state and federal standardized tests and was grouped together, most since kindergarten. The vast majority of the students were the children of teachers or other "professional" (the better term may be working, remember we are talking African Americans in the early to mid-sixties) people throughout the neighborhood. I had been identified as the "bright foster child" that should fit in with the rest of the bright children since I had done well on the tests and was allowed to be in the accelerated program. As our teacher brought her comments to a close she decided to predict the future of her students. She bestowed the title of Doctor, Lawyer, Architect, Corporate Executive, Professor, and Politician to students as she went from desk to desk. Then she got to me, she shook her head, a look of scorn came across her face and said, "And people like Marsialle Arbuckle, well they won't do much in life. If they go to college they'll go to Squatter's University that nobody's ever heard of in Chitlin' Switch, Mississippi somewhere, and end up messing things up where ever they go." The class began to snicker and giggle; a couple of the boys just out right roared with laughter. I glared at the teacher and thought to myself, "I'm going to go to one of the best colleges there is." When I got home from school that day I cried and then forgot about it. But others hadn't forgotten; the first day at the new school, one of the boys that had roared with laughter at the teacher's prediction for my future saw me with a group of others. He came over and said, "Hi Marsialle, how are things at Squatter's U?" He then proceeded to tell the whole story to all the other kids, and the story followed me through to the end of high school.

I must be honest in my recollection and admit that I was a mischievous child and had given that teacher a challenge if not the out and out blues for the entire school year. I would venture to say that's not an excuse for an adult to be so cruel to a child. God's amazing grace once again took control. Another miracle, although I had no economic means to afford it, I attended and graduated from Indiana University. I completed an Associate Degree in Business Studies from the Indiana University School of Business. I also graduated with honors and completed a double major in the areas of Law and Public Policy, and Policy and Administration from Indiana University's School Of Public and Environmental Affairs. Indiana University is a Big Ten school and rated by U.S. News and World Report as one of the top three public institutions of higher learning in America, a far cry from Squatter's University in Chitlin' Switch. My educational blessings did not end there as I was blessed with the opportunity to complete a Masters in Business Management at Central Michigan University. Another testimony to God's Word, **II Corinthians 13:4, For though he was crucified through weakness, yet he liveth by the power of God. For we also are weak in him, but we shall live with him by the power of God toward you.** I must be one of God's chosen ones. Only He could transform a tragedy that could have destroyed the ambition of a young person and devastated the ego and self-esteem of an adolescent into the triumph of achievement and accomplishment. Only God could change a situation to where …**strength is made perfect in weakness.**

Emerson High School Graduation – 1976

Chapter 7

My collegiate experience was tremendously positive. I was blessed with the opportunity to meet great people and develop relationships that would last my entire life. Men that were the son of a doctor, as well as the son of a waiter, as well as the son of a laborer, and the son of an entrepreneur like Frank B. Pace III, Mark E. Artis, Dewayne A. Richardson, John Montgomery, Mark Gibson, and Terrence P. Moore, became my best friends. I became a part of organizations that would mold my outlook on race relations, politics, and facilitate my professional development. I was elected as the first African American in the history of Indiana University to hold the office of First Vice President of the University's Inter-fraternity Council. Little did I know at the time that my relationships with these individuals and others directly associated with those organizations would literally set the direction for my career in the corporate world. As I reflect on the results of my choices for affiliation, my life seems to be a complex symphony; created, directed and conducted by the Master himself.

The fraternal organization that I became a part of is Omega Psi Phi. The fraternity was first revealed to me through our small Christian Methodist Episcopal Church in Gary, Indiana. West Side C.M.E. (The church has since been renamed to Glen Park C.M.E. after it relocated to a larger facility.) Our minster at the time was Rev. H. M. Williamson. Hank as we called him when other adults weren't around was a young dynamic Black man proud of his heritage and strong in his faith. He was just the right mentor/role model for a group of working class or lower middle class youths that stood on the border between socio-economic success and failure, the deciding factor being education. He was linked into Rev. Jesse Jackson and Operation Push, and all of the current activities of the day. His main goal in life seemed to be to motivate the youth of his church to achieve accomplishments never achieved before. One method that he used was to have us repeat the Operation Push motto each week when we had the Christian Youth Fellowship (CYF) meeting. I remember it to this day;

I Am Somebody
I may be Black but;
I Am Somebody;
I may be poor but;
I Am Somebody;
I may be from the ghetto but;
I Am Somebody
I Am Somebody!

That motto fit perfectly with my upbringing as my foster mother Rosie repeatedly would say to my brother Michael and me, "It doesn't matter to me what you do in life, just grow up to Be Somebody!"

Rev. Williamson's second and most important method of encouragement and motivation was through example. He had grown up in Gary's Delaney Housing Project. One of, if not Gary, Indiana's most notorious "Urban" environments. His mother was single and poor but a courageous and hard working woman. Despite these disadvantages, Henry had graduated from high school, and college at the commuter campus of Purdue University, and was enrolled in a master's degree program at Northwestern University in Evanston, IL. In addition he was serving as pastor of our church and working a fulltime job. He accepted no excuses, and he was quick to let you know that he knew all about hard times, and he knew how to get out of them, through hard work. He demonstrated the work ethic needed and reflected the successful results. Rev. Williamson has gone on to become a Bishop of the C.M.E. Church.

The third method of motivation used by the good reverend was public praise for any accomplishment big or small. Only two young men from our church went off to college before my brother Michael, they were Arnold and Roland Massie. When they returned home for Thanksgiving break, Rev. Williamson invited each to speak to the church about their experience. During their presentations, they each had one thing in common; they had both joined Omega Psi Phi while at Purdue University. These two fellows were the most accomplished young men at our church and were guys that I looked up to and wanted to be like. As a result, one of the first things I did when I arrived at Indiana University was to find the men of Omega and seek membership.

Ten years prior to this time, 350 miles away in a different state another young man was joining Omega Psi Phi. Neither he nor I could even imagine at the time that he would be one of the angels designated by God to interact with me, and facilitate one of His many miracles. To ensure that the interaction would take place God touched us both to become a member of the same secret society. We would both learn a phrase; that would identify us to each other and assure us that we should interact and develop a relationship based on Manhood, Scholarship, Perseverance, and Uplift.

The Horn Section – IU Soul Revue – 1979

Chapter 8

I participated in IU commencement exercises during May 1981. I didn't have a good job lined up so I decided to live in the Omega house on campus for the summer. I learned firsthand what adult worries were all about that summer. I had graduated from college; I had no job, no money for graduate school, and no place to go at the end of the summer. While I could return to the home of Walter and Rosie, as their door was always open to me, I felt deep inside that was not the thing to do. They were old, and they had done their part, I needed to face the world on my own, and stand on my own two feet. Using the IU Employment Placement Office as a source for assistance in my job search, daily I would stop in and mail off at least one copy of my resume to a perspective employer. On one such day I forwarded a copy to Ford Motor Company. Of all the Human Resources offices in Ford Motor Company, my resume landed on the desk of Tyrone Havard, Human Resources Manager of Ford's Glass Division.

Tyrone had joined Ford some seven years prior to the arrival of my resume. He was married with two children, and had a budding and bright career future with Ford. His prior work experience had been in Retail Management and Human Resources. Tyrone had read thousands of resumes during his career. It was as if God was providing him with training for the day that he would read the resume of one of "His children". Under usual Ford Motor Company requirements there was nothing about my resume that would have made Mr. Havard select my resume as special based on Ford's preference for engineering majors and his years of experience and training in the field of Human Resources. However, the unique combination of a business management background and a strong curriculum of law, policy, and administration met a special niche that needed to be filled in the area of the Basic Inventory Plan and Warehouse Consignment programs that the Ford Glass Division was offering. There was one other thing that jumped off the page at him as he glanced at the remainder of the resume after focusing on the GPA, and non-engineering course of study. He saw three words that alerted him that this was the resume that God wanted him to finally see after all the resumes that he had reviewed. Omega Psi Phi, Mr. Havard was also a member of Omega Psi Phi Fraternity, Incorporated.

Each member of Omega Psi Phi is taught a special secret phrase. You learn this phrase in an atmosphere of extreme duress. The intent being that you will never forget it no matter how much time has passed or in whatever situation that you are in when you encounter it. As I sat on the 23rd floor of the Detroit Renaissance Center in the corporate suite of Ford Motor

Company, I had no idea that I was about to encounter the phrase. It was as if God had given Mr. Havard a test that he could conduct to assure himself that I was the right person. Never mind the GPA, never mind the non-engineering major, never mind the niche fit, is this person God's chosen recipient of a blessing? The first two times Mr. Havard presented me with the Omega Challenge, I missed it. Had I not caught it the third time Mr. Havard had concluded that he would not present the opportunity that he was prepared to offer. The glorious third time, I began to smile and then laugh as I ask Mr. Havard, "Are you asking what I think you're asking?" He laughed with relief and joy as he told me, "Wow, I was worried that you had misrepresented yourself on the resume and that you really weren't an Omega!" At that point, we left his office and went to lunch, during which time he provided me with the insight and suggestions on how to do well in the interview. Following Mr. Havard's instructions, I performed outstandingly during the interview. Three days later I received an offer for employment from Ford Motor Company that would be one of the highest paying job offers to be received by an IU graduate that year.

Once again God had provided for His child. He had given me an angel that delivered access and opportunity. Access and opportunity that is usually limited to inheritance. Marsialle Arbuckle, a foster child with no connections, receiving the best of the best from the best. **Psalm 116:5-7, Gracious is the Lord, and righteous; yea, our God is merciful. The Lord preserveth the simple: I was brought low, and he helped me. Return unto rest O my soul; for the Lord hath dealt bountifully with thee.** How could I not recognize this as a blessing? How could I do anything but respond as the scriptures suggest? **Psalm**

116:16-17, O Lord, truly I am thy servant; I am thy servant, and the son of thine handmaid: thou hast loosed my bonds. I will offer to thee the sacrifice of thanksgiving, and will call upon the name of the Lord.

Chapter 9

Moving to the metropolitan Detroit area was both exciting and scary for me. While I was about to begin my adult professional life, I was also moving to a big city where I had no friends or relatives. In 1981, the year I relocated, the city of Detroit had the dubious distinction of being the "Murder Capital of the Nation", with more killings per 100,000 people than any other city of comparable size in America. I found another unique trait with the people of Detroit that I had not encountered as an adult, socio-economic class separation within the Black race. I quickly discovered that unless you were properly introduced by a mutual acquaintance, it was difficult to meet people, and all but impossible to really develop a friendship or any other type of relationship.

While a Christian, single, college educated, well employed, heterosexual African American male was as much of an exception in 1981 as he would be today, even that didn't seem to over shadow the apprehension that young ladies felt about dating an "outsider". There were wonderful people all around me, along with great and exciting events occurring all the time. When I attended, it was as if I was there with a button on saying, "Not a Member of the Click". Just four or five weeks of that and Detroit seemed as if it was going to be a miserable and lonely place to live, and then another series of miracles.

First, four African American men that were graduates of Indiana University had obtained positions in the Detroit area, three of which were already my close friends at IU. They were; Frank B. Pace III with IBM, Terrence P. Moore with Xerox, and John Montgomery with Burroughs. Mel Patton a former IU football player that we all knew had also relocated to Detroit to work with Xerox. Upon the arrival of each of my fellow alumni, we immediately made contact and began hanging out and enjoying our new city and home as a team. We shared life as well as work experiences and learned from each other. We shared our successes and failures at work, our successes and failures at developing and maintaining romantic relationships, and we shared discoveries about life and people in general. As a result of Frank's motivation, he and I entered and completed the Central Michigan University Master of Business Management Degree program.

Second, God allowed me to meet and work with Catherine Clark and the Clark family embraced me as a "protégé". Catherine Clark is an African American female salaried retiree of Ford Motor Company. In 1981 she was an analyst with the Ford Glass Division. Cathy had established herself as a knowledgeable and efficient professional and was well respected by all of her co-workers. Cathy was from the "old school" of thinkers when it came to her fellow employees of African descent, one for all, and all for one. When I arrived at

Glass Division, Cathy was proud. She felt proud, happy and excited that a young "brother" had been selected to fill the Ford College Graduate Program slot and she was dedicated to doing everything in her power to make sure that I would be successful. As far as she was concerned, it was critical that I succeed so the opportunity for another was increased. Cathy made it her business to make sure that I had the complete "hook up"; from where to buy business suits at a reasonable price to where to get a good hair cut and not be risking my life. Cathy also invited me to Sunday dinner at her home, "You need to eat at least one wholesome meal a week, to keep you regular." She would smile and say. Cathy and her husband Earl were then and still are true socialites, each meal would include a group of interesting movers and shakers from around the city of Detroit, and the Clarks would provide the "proper introduction". Within a short period of time, I was a member of the in-crowd.

As I reflect on those times, none of the relationships with the "in-crowd" folks seemed to have had very much impact. Oddly enough, one of the most significant and influencing relationships I developed during the time was the result of a chance meeting (or at least at the time I thought it was by chance, now I believe it was all a part of a bigger plan) with an old middle school classmate Kathy Dawson. While walking through a small grocery store in my Detroit suburban community of Southfield, Michigan on a Saturday afternoon, I saw a face that looked so familiar, that I was compelled to say something to the person. I remember laughing to myself as I approached her, because what I was about to say seemed like such a classic "pick-up line", "Excuse me but don't I know you from somewhere, are you Kathy Dawson?"

"Marsialle Arbuckle, is that you?" Kathy responded as we embraced with one of those hugs that you give a long lost friend. "Wow you look so different," Kathy commented as she stepped back to look at me, and she was right. In my earlier teen years, I had been very chubby. In fact who am I kidding, I was a fat kid. Not so huge that I couldn't run and play, just big enough to be slow and clumsy. I was also a great target to be teased and picked at when the future comedians were around. To avert the teasing, I took on a tough guy demeanor whenever it would work. Not the case any longer, I stood before Kathy, as the total package (if I do say so myself). Six foot two inches tall, broad shoulders, narrow at the waist, and a dazzling smile (or sneaky grin) and some believe that my green eyes are attractive.

Kathy's memories of me were from Tolleston Middle School, grades 7 through 9, age 13 through 15, the brutal years. We had played in the band together and were in some classes together. Because we both were high academic achievers, we were grouped in the same scholastic curriculum plan "college prep". During junior high school I was not very popular and Kathy was, she was petite and cute, and everyone seemed to like her. So, while we knew each other fairly well, we weren't what could be described as friends. Kathy was not a person that I had a secret adolescent crush on or anything, in fact she was a part of that unapproachable group of super popular girls, which I couldn't have even fantasized about dating, so I didn't.

The brutal years – circa 1971

Kathy and I exchanged contact information and began communicating and going places together. I describe it as that rather than dating because from the very start Kathy made me aware of her fiancé. He was attending law school in Louisiana and would be coming to Detroit to marry her as soon as he graduated. In my mind I believed that I would overcome that issue with time, but God had other plans. Little did I know that Kathy was one of my assigned angels. Her task was to lead me into an environment that would result in Christian fellowship. One of the places that Kathy wanted to go was to church. While in Detroit I had attended church on several occasions, never joining or getting involved. In fact my last visit to St. John's Christian Methodist Episcopal church resulted in one of life's most embarrassing moments. I arrived at the church and sat on a pew near the rear of the church. Moments later a very distinctively dressed middle-aged woman sat next to me. As the service progressed I noticed that she seemed to be very involved in the service and that she was following along very attentively. Having grown up in the C.M.E. church I was very familiar with the order of worship, the songs being sung and the scriptures recited, which resulted in a pleasant nod from the woman as I sang along without looking at the words in the hymnal. Something that I was not accustomed to was the oratory style used by the minister during his delivery of the sermon. I was use to the yelling and shouting; fire and brimstone method of preaching and this minister was using a soft-spoken lecture approach, which I found totally unacceptable. Feeling that I had established a slight camaraderie with the woman sitting next to me, I leaned over to her and whispered, "This guy must by kidding, I can't believe he calls this delivering a sermon, he just can't preach!" She looked at me with a horrified glare of disdain and whispered back, "No, I didn't think that but, I'll be sure to tell my husband, the minister up there, how you feel." How was I to know that she was the pastor's wife! Needless to say I shrank into my seat, and after the service was over I scurried away never to return.

The church that I most often attended, with or without Kathy, was Hartford Memorial Baptist Church. I really enjoyed the services, the choirs were fantastic, the preacher Rev. Charles G. Adams was an outstanding orator, and the church had numerous social outreach programs. I felt helping the community was one of the key missions of the church, and Hartford did a tremendous job of it. While I did not join the church, I did participate by helping Mr. Havard, my mentor and a member of the church, coach a youth basketball team. The Christian fellowship that Kathy had helped to lead me to made my life complete and fulfilled.

Another impact that my relationship with Kathy had was more subtle with longer lasting positive effects. Kathy restored my faith in the concept of true love and commitment. From our first encounter and throughout the remaining years, Kathy maintained her commitment to the Louisiana lawyer. During those days, many of the young women that I dated were very superficial with no loyalty at all. The focus seemed to be more on what you did for a living, how much money you made, what type of car you drove, and the prevailing attitude was, I'll trade you in for a better model whenever the opportunity presents itself.

While I was in undergrad at Indiana University I had become engaged to my college sweetheart. After graduation and my move to Detroit we broke off the engagement because we both couldn't refrain from seeing other people. In her case, she started dating a guy she had met during a visit to me in Detroit. The irony of that incident left me with a diminished opinion of women. That added to my emotional baggage from being abandoned by my mother, and left me in quite a fragile emotional state with regards to women. To be honest, I didn't hold women in very high esteem at all. Just as I had gotten to the point of becoming a product of my environment and developing the same type of attitude and behavior as I was encountering, God brought Kathy into my life and she restored my faith in romance, love, and even marriage. I wanted to have someone as committed to me as she was to that guy. Kathy's devotion to her long distance love, made me believe that Ms. Right was out there, I just had to find her. Kathy ultimately married the gentleman and they have a lovely home and three beautiful children.

Chapter 10

After four years, two promotions, and obtaining a Master's degree, Ford Motor Company decided they needed my services in another location; Claremore, Oklahoma. The Ford Glass Division had constructed a small fabricating plant, in a little town 30 miles outside of Tulsa, Oklahoma. It happens to be the hometown of 1950's western film star and philanthropist Will Rogers. In the mid-1980's Claremore had 3 stoplights on the main street, U.S. Route 6. You could literally drive through the town and never stop, by passing it completely if the three lights were synchronized to green simultaneously. The management decided that I would not relocate to the facility; rather travel there for two or three week stints and then return. If the issues could be addressed in a few visits, there would be no need for me to permanently relocate. Since there were no hotels in Claremore, I would reside in Tulsa and commute daily to Claremore.

This arrangement resulted in a "plum" assignment for me. I enjoyed the travel and the excitement of going someplace new and exploring another part of the country. Airfare, room charges, food, and a car to drive with the gasoline to put in it; even laundry, valet and haircuts were charged to my expense account. That resulted in me building a financial base with the money that I saved. Things seemed to be going great! I was meeting nice people; one family in particular was the Hooks'. I had met Renee Hooks while out and about in Tulsa one evening. We developed a great relationship that led to me meeting her family. Her mother invited me to church and after learning that they were members of a C.M.E. Church, I accepted the invitation and attended with them on a regular basis. Life was grand, and then the phone call.

I was sitting at the desk in Claremore one afternoon and the phone rang. It was my brother Michael. "Marsialle, I've found our mother," Michael said in an exasperated voice. "Man I've found Augustine!" He went on to tell me the story of how he had gone to a local florist in Indianapolis, Indiana where he lived to get flowers for his wife. How shocked the florist was after he told her his name to put on the receipt. Michael told me how she responded that it was an unusual name which she had recently encountered for the first time when visiting a lady in a nursing home with a group from her church. Michael told me how shocked he was when the florist said that the woman's name was *Augustine* Arbuckle. After 27 years, Michael had found our biological mother, but that's not all.

"And guess what man, we got a sister and another brother that we didn't know about," Michael said with joy. "What?" I replied with total amazement. "That's right man; we got a little half sister and brother. I've hooked up with our sister; she's coming to 'Nap' tomorrow for a visit. Man momma looks just like you, you're gonna trip out! You gotta come to Nap-Town this weekend cause there's gonna be a big reunion and the TV news, newspaper, and magazine people are gonna be there. This is a big-ass deal ya know." The speed and volume of Michael's voice had increased to nearly screams, as his apparent excitement was sincere and escalating. "Slow down, hold up, what do you mean a reunion, I asked?" "Well, when the people at the home heard about what was going on they called the Indianapolis Star. When they found out we were from Gary they contacted the Gary Post Tribune. The people at the Tribune helped me locate our sister and now it's a bigger story and they want to cover the reunion. Finding your roots is the in thing now ya know." "Home, what home?" I inquired. "Let me start over from the beginning," Michael said as I could tell he was making an effort to calm down so he could give me the details.

Augustine and Willie Jr. had gone on a mini crime spree immediately after their abandonment of the three of us, which led to their eventual incarceration. Apparently Augustine and Willie Jr. went their separate ways after that. Her sentence was a short one, and upon her return to Gary she met a man, fell in love and they had two children, a son and daughter, Robert and Royletta. They too were raised in foster homes from a very young age. Once again Augustine's addictions had taken control of her actions and she got herself incarcerated again, this time for a bit longer. She received an early parole with conditions that included she could never return to Gary, Indiana. So, she took residence in Indianapolis, and started working at the Indianapolis Star Newspaper. Shortly after she began her new job at the newspaper, she had a severe stroke. The effects of the stroke combined with her large size debilitated and basically immobilized her. Since she was still on parole and a ward of the state of Indiana, after hospitalization, she was placed in the Marion County Convalescence Center. She had been there for the last eight or nine years.

Michael said he had been to visit her everyday and had asked her some questions that he always wanted to know the answer to. Like why had they left us, but before he could go on I stopped him. My mind was racing, and I was at work. I didn't want to open that can at the office, so I changed the focus of our discussion without changing the subject. "So what does our sister look like?" "I don't know, I won't see her 'til this weekend, she's coming for the reunion." Michael and I ended the conversation with me giving him a busy office excuse to go, along with a promise for a call later and to see him on Friday. I didn't keep either promise.

I didn't want my first visit with Augustine after 20 years to be part of a media spread on the human-interest section of the Sunday newspaper. At least that's what I convinced myself of and used as rationale to Michael. There were so many other thoughts that worked to my most inner being. There was rage and fury on one end of the spectrum, to curiosity and instinctive love on the other end. There was disdain and disgust accompanied by sympathy and pity. And there was the reality of the situation and circumstance. A situation so simple, yet circumstances so extremely complex.

- Simple- Your mother whom you haven't seen in over 20 years is just a flight away, go see her and hug her and kiss her!

- Complex- Your mother who abandons you when you were just 2 years old is just a flight away, go tell her about it. Tell her that if you abandon a two-year-old, you basically are leaving it to die because a two-year-old can't possibly care for itself.

- Simple- Your mother whom you haven't seen in over 20 years is just a flight away, go see her and tell her what a big success you are and how proud she can be of you.

- Complex- Your mother who abandoned you when you were just 2 years old is just a flight away, go tell her how you succeeded despite her leaving you and your brothers on that cold afternoon. Tell her how you overcame the odds. How you withstood the children's teasing and teachers torment in school because you were a foster child!

- Simple- Your mother whom you haven't seen in over 20 years is just a flight away, go see her and tell her how happy you are to meet your little sister and brother.

- Complex- Your mother who abandons you when you were just 2 years old is just a flight away, go ask her how could she have done the same thing twice? How could she abandon two more children and have them grow up in the foster care system also?

- Simple- Your mother whom you haven't seen in over 20 years is just a flight away, go see her and tell her how you've missed her hugs and words of comfort during your struggle.

- Complex- Your mother who abandons you when you were just 2 years old is just a flight away, go and tell her that the hugs and comfort that you needed from a mother was and is still being fully provided by your God appointed mother, who is named Rosie Yearby.

The next few days went by quickly and the week ended with me staying in Oklahoma. That Sunday as I had done for the last 10 years, I called Rosie. Before I could finish saying hello, she laid it on the line, she was always very direct. "Mike called and said he found your momma in a home down there in Indianapolis. They're having a big reunion. Are you there in Indianapolis with them?" "Nope," I replied, "I didn't want to be a part of the media circus, and it's just going to be a lot of reporters, cameras, and pictures and putting on. I don't need that mess." "Don't you want to see your momma Marsialle?" "I'm talking to my momma right now, and I'll be there to see you in a couple of weeks." There was a silence, short if you had to time it, but an eternity at the moment, and then, "You're a good boy Marsialle, you're a good boy."

I stuck to my rationale of media avoidance, which Michael accepted without much fuss. Our brothers Montclair and Robert could not be located so the reunion event was not as grand as intended. Within a few days Michael mailed me a copy of the article that had been generated; it made reference to me as "another one of Ms. Arbuckle's sons is an auto industry executive that resides in Detroit, Michigan." The acknowledgement made me smile when I considered that I hadn't yet reached a management role at Ford Motor Company at the time. The remainder of the article chronicled the event and gave it a "and they all lived happily ever after ending". It wasn't the end, nor was it all happy, but the "ever after" part is accurate.

Chapter 11

Three to four weeks after the big reunion I had an opportunity to go to Indiana. My friend Mark Artis was about to get married and I had been asked to be one of the groomsmen in the wedding. I decided that I would conduct my visit with Augustine on Saturday morning before the wedding. Friday night was the big bachelor party at a suite in the hotel we were all staying in. The party lasted until the wee hours. I attempted to lie down afterward but I couldn't sleep. I went out and walked about the grounds and parking lot of the hotel contemplating my pending meeting. How would I say hello. Would I hug her, or shake hands. What would we talk about, should I talk about me or her? As the sun began to rise I went back inside. There was Mark walking through the lobby of the hotel. "Hey man, what the hell are you doing up so early?" I asked. "Buckeroo-Whoodi-Who…man I can't sleep, these are the last hours of my life," Mark said with a roar of laughter. "But what are you doing up at this hour?" "Well, I can't sleep either, I've got something pretty important to do today before the wedding myself." I guess Mark could tell by the look on my face and the sound of the tone of my voice that I was serious. His next move was unexpected but as I look back, oh so necessary. "Well, Whoodi-Who, let's go to my room, I'm shining my shoes, you ever done a military spit-shine before?"

As we entered Mark's suite, I could see he was serious about the shoeshine. Rags, polish, and a brush were on the counter. Mark went to work on his shoes and started telling a bit of his life story, how he had gone to military school for a few years, and hated it. He did however learn how to do the military spit-shine, which he was applying to his wedding shoes. Mark then asked me a very unexpected question, "Buck, we've been friends for over six or seven years, and you're one of the few people who really know me as an adult, whose opinion I respect. Do you think I'm doing the right thing, you know, getting married and to Alice and all?" I was shocked that Mark actually wanted to know my opinion, but I was also more than willing to give it. "Look Mark, you and Alice have been together for awhile now, and you've had plenty of time to decide if you're right for each other. You love her, and more importantly she's absolutely crazy for you. It's perfect!" As I looked at Mark I was astonished that I saw a tremendously sincere look of relief and gratitude on his face. If I didn't know better, I thought that had my opinion been the opposite, he would have been devastated. I did know better, but it's great to feel that your opinion is truly respected. "Thanks Whoodi, I just wanted to know what you thought," Mark smiled and continued his spit-shine.

The sincerity in Mark's inquiry and response helped me to open up to him, and I really needed to just talk to someone that would listen and reserve opinion. I shared with him what was to occur in the next few hours. I told him how conflicted my emotions were and that the mere fact I was conflicted created even more mental anguish and turmoil. I told him how I loved and adored Rosie and that I was committed to her as a parent no matter what. I told Mark about my anger and resentment toward Augustine. I shared with Mark the guilt and regret that I felt for the feeling of anger that I felt toward another human being. I told him how the guilt intensified when I considered the fact that my disdain was toward my own biological mother. Mark listened, polished, and listened. On occasion, he would look up, with a raised eyebrow or a wrinkled brow. Mark never said anything beyond um or wow. When it was apparent that I was done, Mark broke his silence, "Well Whoodi, you gotta get it done and you done tougher stuff, so you'll make it!" I knew then that there was nothing else to be said about the circumstances, I just needed to deal with the situation.

I dressed in a light tan gabardine and wool blend business suit, white button down collar shirt, silk paisley patterned brown necktie, and dark brown Bostonian shoes. Each strand of hair on my head was in its proper place and my mustache was trimmed to perfection. My fingernails were clean and clipped, my college graduation ring on the fourth finger of my left hand and a gold Wittenuaer watch on the left wrist. My external appearance was impeccable and above reproach; I had no idea what I looked like internally. As I drove up in front of the facility the sterile solitude of institutionalized living began to impact me. Everything from the grounds to the building, even the smell reflected, "You're in the system." The walls were white and sanitary; the few pictures that hung were impersonal landscapes and florals. As I approached the front desk, it seemed as if things shifted into slow motion. Each step seemed to land with a loud boom. Each stride long and slow, even my voice, "Helloooooooo, I'mmmmmmmmm herrrrreee tooooooo seeeeeee Auggggggggguuuuuustine Arrrrrrrrbucklllllllleeee." "Are you her son? She's been expecting you, I'll tell her you're here." With the sound of the receptionist's voice, I snapped out of it.

As I walked down the corridor to her room I practiced my greeting; "Hi, I'm Marsialle." Not "Hi Mom, it's me your baby boy"; no emotional outcry; no physical contact; strictly business and professional. I stepped through the door and there she was a female version of Michael, she looked just like him. The years of life showed through, but they were not the look of hard years. More like the look of years of illness. Although she was huge in dimension, she seemed frail and weak. Her eyes immediately evoked pity and sympathy, but there was no overwhelming instinctive sense of love or attachment that I had expected. "Hi, I'm Marsialle, it's nice to meet you," I said with a smile and a nod. "It's nice to meet you too sir," she replied with a humble respect one would think reserved for the most esteemed person an individual might encounter. "Well uh, do you mind if I come in and have a seat?" "No sir, I don't mind," she said in the same humble tone. I looked around the room, and spotted a chair in the corner. I pulled it to the bedside and sat down.

"Well, uh you probably know a lot more about me than I know about me, so I guess I'd like to start off by asking you some questions if it's ok?" "No sir, I don't mind," she replied. "You don't have to address me as or call me sir," I responded.

"Michael and the others have told me what an important man you are and everything," I held up my hand and stopped her, "Michael likes to blow things out of proportion sometimes, I'm not anybody important, and I just have a decent job that's all. Tell me, how did you come up with my name, where does Marsialle DuShant come from?" "Well I got it from the stories on TV." Augustine went on to tell me that there was a famous French artist around the time that I was born, named Marseille Du Shant. He came up with what she described as some kind of new looking pictures and they talked about him and his pictures a lot on television. Since she watched it all the time, she named me after him. I remember thinking to myself that I had never heard of an artist of note with that name, but that I would try and look him up later. After an hour or more of the pleasantries the burning question came to mind, and I dropped the boom. I asked, "How could you leave us like that?" Her eyes shifted downward, and the room fell silent, then "We didn't leave ya'll, we turned ya'll into the welfare, and then they wouldn't give ya'll back. I thought that I was doing the best by ya'll. I gave ya'll a better chance in life by leaving ya'll with those nice people, and look at you."

Her words cut like a hot knife through butter. How could she fabricate a story? At this point why would she lie? They did not turn us in. I have never figured it out, all be it I've tried. Maybe she couldn't face the fact that she had committed such a horrendous deed. Maybe she had blanked it out in her mind and convinced herself that it happened differently in order to be able to live with herself. Maybe she just couldn't face her victim and admit the mistreatment. Regardless, she was justifying the action based on a positive outcome. She was focusing on the outcome of the situation and not the circumstances surrounding it. I decided not to have a confrontation; rather, I changed the focus of our discussion without changing the subject.

My next question was as difficult for me to ask, as it seemed for her to answer. I ask her why she had never attempted to contact us, especially since she knew where we were. Her responses made sense and were reasonable. "I did once, but it was so hard on your brother Michael that I promised that lady, you-all's foster momma, that I'd never bother ya'll again. Then the state fixed it so I couldn't contact ya'll without breaking the law." There was a deep pain in her voice, a pain that only years of suffering could yield. But, because of my distant relationship and my state of being, I could only hear her pain, but I could not feel her pain. There was pain in my heart, but my suffering was my own. It was not shared through a common bond that somehow should have existed between Augustine and I, between mother and son. My pain was solitary, personal and intense. It was at that point I pulled from the strength that God had provided me throughout the years. The grace that had been saving, sustaining and sufficient for years gone by totally embodied my being and my pain transformed into a ubiquitous calm.

At that point I began wrapping up our visit, and I decided that I would be forthright in stating my disposition regarding the entire matter. I shared with Augustine that I had done well so far in life and that childhood with the Yearby's had been just fine. Although I had suffered the stigma of being a foster child, I had gotten over it. Mr. and Mrs. Yearby had given me everything a youngster growing up could need and most of the things that I wanted. I told her that there was only one thing that was missing that she could have provided, and it wasn't too late for her to provide it now because I would always need it, friendship and love. I told her that Rosie had and still provides the mother's love that I needed, and that she couldn't just tell me that she loved me, Augustine, I told her, "You'll have to show me that you love me." I told Augustine that she could show me by becoming my friend, because it was too late for a parent-child relationship. It was just the little things that I desired, like a card on my birthday or a call at Christmas. As I stood to leave we looked at each other eye to eye and then she said "Thank you sir." I replied, "Please, don't call me sir, I'm just Marsialle."

Chapter 12

As I drove away from the facility that morning I decided that the only way I was going to maintain my sanity about the situation was that I had to keep the associated circumstances in their proper perspective. I could not judge Augustine and Willie Jr. *Their* decisions had led *them* to a point where *they* took an action. *They* did what *they* felt *they* had to do at the time. I, nor my existence, did not cause *them* to make the decision or take the action, and my resulting situation was simply a byproduct of *their* decisions and actions. There is but one ultimate authority that will pass judgment on their decisions and actions. I on the other hand stood just as they, in a position to do what I felt I had to do. What I felt I had to do was to keep moving forward with my life. Not allow myself to get caught-up emotionally or ideologically. I had to use my energy to continue to take advantage of the opportunities that God was providing me. I knew that God had provided this opportunity and I had to utilize it because it had to be a part of God's plan, and I knew His plans were for the good of all involved. **Romans 8:28, And we know that all things work together for good to them that love God, to them who are the called according to *his* purpose.**

Earlier in the week leading up to the wedding an old proverb had been shared with me during a phone call with an acquaintance:

Luck - when preparation meets opportunity.

I found that simple definition to be profound, accurate, and directly applicable to my life. The positive and good things that had occurred in my life were without question linked to my being prepared as opportunities became available to me. From being Drum Major in the high school marching band because I was the only band member that knew his routine step for step on the day he was too ill to perform, to being hired by Ford Motor Company because when my resume landed on the desk of a fraternity brother, I had the right academic training and achievement to meet the qualifications for employment. I therefore decided that proverb would be my motto and creed. I committed to be prepared to take advantage of any and all opportunities that God sent my way. I'm sure that conversation also influenced my thinking and helped to provide me with the mental toughness to deal with the situation despite my "hang-ups" and issues.

As I reflect back, I believe that God's purpose may have been to use me as more of a blessing for Augustine rather than her being a blessing for me. Psalm 116 teaches us that we are obligated to give as we have received and share our love and blessings the same way that God has dealt with us despite our unworthiness. I was wrong to ask Augustine to prove that she loved me. I did nothing more to deserve the love of God than to exist. Why should I ask that she deserve my love and assistance? I pray for God's mercy and forgiveness of my arrogance. I should have viewed her as Jesus viewed the masses of helpless people in Matthew 9:37, as a plentiful harvest, a harvest of opportunity. I now know that people are not problems to be rejected but possibilities to be fulfilled. I know that I must have love especially for those that seem hopeless and unworthy.

As I dressed in the tuxedo for the wedding I cleared my mind of the events of the past couple of hours. While I stood at the altar with six of my best friends I was completely removed from the other half of the dual edged circumstances that had me in the situation of being in Indianapolis. Alice was a beautiful bride and Mark a handsome groom. The wedding was grand and the reception even better. That reception would be the last time that I saw Timmy Grant. The circumstances that surround the situation involving his death were so horrible; a novel could be dedicated to the issue. I pray that God will rest his soul in peace.

I left the reception early to face my second life enhancing event of the day, a visit to Michael and to meet my little sister for the first time at age 26. As I walked up the sidewalk to Michael's front door I wondered what my sister would be like. How did she smile, talk, walk, who was she? Would she be a pleasant person, high energy or low key? I knocked at the door and she opened it. Once again my eyes beheld a female version of Michael. I guess if you see a reflection of yourself in the mirror, and you don't know who that person is, you relate them to someone else you know that looks similar. Others will say that Royletta looks like me, that I look like Augustine, that Augustine looks like Montclair, that Montclair looks like Michael, and so on. The bottom line was that we all have a distinctive family genetic similarity of appearance that we were not aware of because we had not all seen each other as adults before.

Mercedes Royletta Leason was her name at the time (she has since married) and what a wonderful person she was to meet. Don't worry be happy seemed to be her words to live by. She had the fast pace energy of a person in their early adulthood. The world was full of possibilities and she was going after her share of the good ones. I was shocked to learn that she had moved to Indianapolis after her visit to the reunion. She actually never returned to Gary from the visit. She had married her high school sweetheart and had recently become a widow. Her late husband had been the victim of an accident at work on his railroad job. She therefore had no reason to remain in Gary and was looking forward to starting a new life in what she called the metropolis of Indianapolis. I was even more shocked to learn that she was living with Michael until she got "established."

I nearly had to bite my lip to keep from bursting with laughter as l observed the strained look in Mike's eyes as he nodded in agreement and acceptance of the plan. He was already feeling the strain of a new sibling in the nest. I could tell they were going to be the "odd couple," and from early indications of Royletta's personality, she seemed to have any upper hand that may have existed. Another astounding fact of the evening was when Royletta revealed that she had known of me during our high school years. That she had attended the same high school at the same time as I. She shared with me how she would come and watch me perform as drum major during marching band practices from behind the football stadium bleachers. Why wouldn't you come and introduce yourself and meet me I asked. "You just seemed bigger than life and I was afraid," Royletta replied in a tone that revealed the vulnerability of an adolescent dealing with the complex circumstances surrounding the simple issue of abandonment and the foster childcare system.

My visit that evening with Royletta and Michael was rather short. I didn't ask her a lot of questions about her childhood or past. My mind had processed enough already and I had a two-hour drive to Gary, Indiana early the next morning. It was enough to meet her and discover that my little sister was a wonderful person. I left them and returned to the hotel. As I pondered the events of the day my mind seemed to run from thought to thought. I began rethinking each word of my conversation with Augustine and Royletta. I started to see their faces on my eyelids as I attempted to close my eyes for sleep. Faces that I had never seen before but yet were so familiar. I finally asked for rest and God granted my prayer with a peace and calm that only he could provide. I slept like a rock for the rest of the night. **Philippians 4:7, And the peace of God, which passeth all understanding, shall keep your hearts and minds through Christ Jesus.**

Chapter 13

Driving along I-65 at 7:30 a.m. can be as calming as anything one could ever imagine. The Indiana plains were golden and brownish green as cornfields and wheat fields rolled by for mile after mile. In 1983 there are only a few large cities between Gary and Indianapolis along I-65, Lafayette, Indiana being the largest. Once again my mind was racing. Not so much on the events of the day before but on the upcoming events on this dawning day. I would be visiting Rosie and Walter. My itinerary for the day included attending church with her and then having an early dinner after church before getting on the road again. Then it would be I-94 directly to Detroit. I would get one night with my Detroit girlfriend, and then on a flight to Oklahoma first thing Monday morning.

First there would be the bragging on me at church. While my ego loved it, I must admit that it was a bit embarrassing. Rosie had been told early on in her guardianship of us that she was too old to manage the rearing of two boys. Public opinion (her fellow church members) felt that it would be like someone's great grandmother attempting to rear children. It was pointed out to her that there would be a generation gap and that she would not be capable of meeting our developmental needs during our adolescent and teen years. She wouldn't know how to talk to us, or keep up with us, or control us.

Marsialle Arbuckle was living evidence that her doubters were wrong. I was proof positive that not only was she capable of completing the task, but that she also could outperform those that had cast doubt. This meant that during each of my visits home I was required to accompany her to any and all church events so she could "Show them a thing or two about raisin' kids and how to train 'em up to be somebody!" Rosie would grin and say "Forgive me Lord," immediately following such self-indulgent proclamations.

After church there would be dinner, which would consist of my favorite dish, beef pot roast. The cut of beef set aside specially for this meal by her personal butcher at the meatpacking house in Hobart, Indiana. Rosie had been a customer there for years and had a friendship with the butcher. Her preparation of the roast reflected years of experience. The taste and tenderness revealed culinary secrets that only time and repetition could render. Also there would be candied sweet potatoes, smothered cabbage and cornbread made from scratch. Desert would be peach or blueberry cobbler, with homemade ice cream à la mode.

As I continued to drift into the nostalgia of life with Rosie and Walter while driving along, I began to recall a situation in which the circumstances seemed overwhelming, but the love and togetherness of a couple working as a team took control of the situation. I was around the age of 7 or 8 years old. Time had spawned advancement. Gary, Indiana was developed and so was our neighborhood. The streets had been paved, and homes dotted both sides of our entire block as well as throughout the community. The city had installed water and sewage systems that made the wells and septic tanks in backyards obsolete. Natural gas pipelines were laid, and homeowners replaced oil and coal furnaces with new cleaner burning natural gas furnaces. Technological and equipment advancements had occurred also; there was now color television along with refrigerators that contained icemakers in the door. At the workplace, advancement meant a new challenge for Walter. There was new equipment for Walter to operate, but he couldn't read the instructions. If he couldn't remedy the situation quickly he would be fired.

Walter worked the midnight shift as a forklift driver. He would leave for work around 10:30 p.m. when we were in bed and arrive home each morning just as we were to have our breakfast before Michael and I left for school. As was the custom at most meals, we sat at the kitchen table with full place settings. Rosie believed in doing things in a "proper and dignified" fashion. As we ate our meal Walter would tell his wife about the events of the previous night. He would speak mostly about incidents of discrimination or about injuries, which seemed to occur with regularity as I recall. On this morning Walter was both disgusted and angry. Walter said that the plant had received new forklifts for them to operate with lots of buttons, knobs, switches, and levers. The operating instructions were adhered to the machines and he couldn't read them and therefore he couldn't operate the piece of equipment. He said that his white counter parts were looking and laughing and wouldn't show him a thing. "They want me to get fired so they can get one of their good 'ole boys in the spot," Walter said to Rosie in a near defeated voice. Her reply, "Don't worry about it baby, we'll figure out something this evening. You're just tired now so eat up and get some rest, and I'll pray about it." Her voice was both calm and reassuring. "You boys finish up now, it's time for you to get going so you're not late," Rosie squawked at Michael and me. We knew her tone meant that we were to finish in silence and not attempt to enter the "grown folks talk" that was occurring. That night as we were in bed I could hear Rosie and Walter developing their plan, even though I didn't understand it at the time. "Make sure you remember your pencil is in the sandwich, and take your time," were Rosie's final instructions as Walter left for work that night.

The next morning, as Walter arrived, he and Rosie immediately went into the dining room and spread two large sheets of paper out on the table. They began going over the papers with excitement and laughter. Although Walter couldn't write, he had used his ingenuity to draw and trace the layout of the forklift panel and the figures (words), as he referred to them on the instructions panel. Walter's detailed diagram enabled Rosie to read the operating instructions to him. Together as a team they had overcome a tremendous obstacle. This obstacle could have had a horribly negative impact on their lives, as well as on the lives of my brother and me. There was no finger pointing, or casting of blame. None of that banter about "Doing bad by myself," from Rosie or "If it hadn't been for you holding me back," from Walter, just prayer and planning. I smiled as I compared their response to the situation and the accompanying circumstances to the tradition of the four cardinal principles of my fraternity, Omega Psi Phi. Rosie displayed uplift and scholarship, while in the face of extreme pressure; Walter had embodied the definition of manhood and perseverance.

I turned the corner from 23rd Avenue onto the 22nd block of Arthur Street and rolled up to the small white two-bedroom bungalow with a carport on the north end. As usual the grass was green and neatly trimmed. The sidewalk edges were lined with flowers, which were predominantly red, white, or purple petunias. As always, Rosie was waiting and watching for my arrival and was standing at the doorway as I strolled up the walkway to the front door.

She was dressed as I expected her to be on the first Sunday of the month. She wore a white nurse's dress with a pink handkerchief pinned to the upper left side, which was the uniform for the Missionaries and Stewardess' Societies at the church. Rosie was a rather small woman, a size eight or ten dress. Her complexion was on the lighter end of the spectrum for African Americans, but tanned to a golden light brown, the result of countless hours in the sun while gardening, walking or fishing; three of her favorite pastimes. Rosie's silver gray wig was properly placed atop her head. I'm sure she never knew of the teasing Michael and I participated in with our neighborhood buddies regarding her variety of wigs or her Sunday hair as she called it. Each week she would neatly pin a different wig atop a Styrofoam manikin head and place it in what looked like an oversized hatbox. She would then carry it across the street to her friend Mrs. Lynch a beautician, to have it curled and set. The 'ole gang would get such a laugh at the thought, even though it made perfectly good sense for her to do so.

"Hi Mommy," I said as I entered. Rosie reached up and greeted me with a warm hug. I was nearly two feet taller than she was now and I reached down and pinched her on the cheek, "Stop that boy," she said with a smile and slapped at my hand with a love tap. "Where's Daddy?" I inquired as I noticed that his "Lazy Boy" sleeper chair was empty, his regular post when in the house. "He's out back in the garden pulling some tomatoes to give to Sister Howard when we get to church," Rosie replied in a matter of fact tone. It was in that same tone she began her inquiry about my first visit with Augustine and my sister Royletta later that day after church during dinner.

I gave Rosie every detail of the conversation I had held with Augustine. I recreated the scene of our meeting and covered each topic that Augustine and I had discussed. Rosie listened intensely but made no comment, which I found unusual. She seemed to stare at me deeply, looking for some level of emotion that I was attempting to conceal or control. After it was evident that I had completed the story, she asked me to recount my meeting with Royletta. I did so in the same detailed fashion that I had covered my meeting with Augustine. Rosie finally broke her silence, "I talked to your brother Michael this morning, and he's just eating your momma up. Seems like he's just crazy about her." I looked up from my plate at her, and there it was, an attitude or I guess you could call it an emotion that I had never seen in Rosie in our 25 or so year relationship. She was scorned and jealous. I responded with the only thing that I could think to say that would both comfort and reassure her, "Well you're the only mother that I'm crazy about. I'd eat you up but I'm too full from this good dinner now." Walter grunted out a laughing tone as I thought of how to change the topic without changing the subject. "Besides you know how fickle Michael is, he'll meet some new girlfriend and forget all about her, I hope he doesn't start something he doesn't finish with all this visiting everyday that he's doing right now." "My sister seems like she's a real nice person," I quickly blurted out to switch topics on this subject. It worked, the conversation drifted and we finished desert without much fanfare.

I prepared to leave Gary early that afternoon, immediately following dinner. I stood on the front porch of the house with Rosie at my side. She took my hand and said that we should pray together before I left. I said ok and we reentered the house and went to the corner in the living room that was reserved for prayer and bowed to our knees. Without a request, Walter turned off the television and went outside. He was not one to participate, but also never hindered Rosie in her religious expression.

I can recall the words of that prayer so clearly, as I've heard it or various portions of it throughout my entire life and interface with the Black church. Her delivery was unique, inasmuch as she used the same words, but not the dialect or rhythmic chant most often utilized by African Americans when praying. Rosie rather prayed in a tone that was businesslike and matter of fact.

> **Lord, here it is once more and again that your meek and humble servant is knee bent and body bowed; Lord I didn't bow here in any shape, form, or fashion, neither nor to be an outside show to this unfriendly world.**

Father I bowed here to say thanks to you. Thank you for waking me up this morning clothed in my right mind.

My mattress was not my cooling board and the comforter was not my winding-sheet. Thank you!

I cast my eyes to the East and I saw the sun rising on the horizon and I say, thank you!

I listened carefully and I could hear the birds singing sweetly in the trees and I thank you!

Father I stretch my hand to thee for no other help I know.

I ask you to bless the sick and afflicted here and elsewhere, and let the prison bound please be thy Holy will.

I ask you to bless my friends and my enemies, and everyone under the sound of my voice.

Lord you know my heart and my heart's desires. I ask you to bless my family.

Especially my husband, make him strong where he is weak and build him up where he is torn down.

Please bless my two sons Michael and Marsialle.

Throw your loving arms of protection around them, and keep them, and give them the desire and self-discipline to follow your Holy Word.

Be with Marsialle as he travels the highways and airways, show him your traveling mercy.

Now Lord I ask you to bless me. Heal my body; help me to carry my burdens, for my heart is heavy.

Give ease to my weary soul, and soothe my troubled mind.

Lord you are a doctor that has never lost a patient,
for there is more healing power in the hem of your
garment than in all the laboratories scientist can
create.
God you are my heart fixer and mind regulator, for
it is you that binds my broken heart and eases the
pain of my afflictions.
Now Lord when I have come to the end of
my journey and I take off the breastplate of
righteousness, lay my shield down by the riverside
and stick my sword in the sands of time, I ask you
to meet me on the other side of that river of Jordan
and greet me with the words; well done, well done
my good and faithful servant well done. I pray this
prayer in the matchless name of thy son Jesus Christ
and ask that you help teach us the prayer that you
taught your disciples to say... (At this point I joined
in)...
Our Father, which art in heaven,
Hallowed be thy name.
Thy kingdom come.
Thy will be done, on earth as it is in heaven.
Give us this day our daily bread.
And forgive us our trespasses, as we forgive those
who have trespassed against us.
And lead us not into temptation, but deliver us from
evil.
For thine is the kingdom, and the power, and the
glory, forever. Amen.

I and Rosie

Chapter 14

The next several months seemed to fly by uneventfully, and then with all the corporate fanfare associated with such occasions, I received another promotion. This time the promotion was my dream come true, the assignment I had been praying for. I was to be the new Field Sales Representative in the Chicago office. I felt, and correctly, like God was blessing me so bountifully. However, the focus of my thoughts was shallow and self-absorbed. I thought to myself that I was being given the opportunity to make a triumphant return home. I felt it was an opportunity to show everyone from my past how big time and successful I had become. I would soon learn that God had a totally different and much nobler purpose for answering my prayers. Rather than being the blessed, I was to become the blessing, and being a blessing isn't easy.

My relocation to the Chicago area was swift. I selected what was in my opinion a luxury apartment in Palos Hill, Illinois to live. The complex was located southwest of downtown Chicago better known as the Loop. My apartment was situated two miles from the entrance ramp of several expressways. First the I-294 toll-way which led to Wisconsin, I-55 which led to the southern half of the state, I-80 which led to Iowa, and I-94 which led to Indiana. All of these highways ended in downtown Chicago's Loop. My new home was also 31 miles or a 30-minute drive from Gary, which would facilitate daily visits to Rosie and Walter.

My new work assignment was challenging. I was one of sixteen individuals selected by Ford to sell its excess supply of glass. The company manufactured glass for its use in the assembly of automobiles. The production capacity exceeded Ford's requirements so we sold the surplus product on the open market. Since glass is a commodity, we had the responsibility to negotiate pricing based on market conditions. That's the means by which I became a savvy businessman with good negotiating skills. Doing business in the Chicago market is tough to say the least. One must be intuitive and alert or you'll find yourself or the firm you represent the victim of a bad deal or agreement.

The fringe benefits of the new assignment were great. Included was a company car with the gas to go in it. I was allowed to fill the gas tank at anytime during the week, and to "top-off" the tank on Fridays before midnight. We were provided with a corporate credit card that had a $25,000 limit. We were allotted the $25,000 as an expense account for entertainment and travel each year, along with season tickets for several professional sports teams, including the Chicago Cubs, the Chicago White Sox, and the Chicago Bulls. Since Michael Jordan was at the prime of his career, access to Chicago Bulls tickets made me very popular. In addition we were allocated $10,000 worth of merchandising aids. Things like ink pens, tee shirts, baseball caps, golf balls, address and date books, calendars, or anything that you could put the Ford logo along with your name and phone number on. If you want to be the big man in the eyes of a receptionist, and always allowed to see the boss without the proper appointment, just have a nice little trinket or bobble to hand him or her. I found that the 10-karat gold Cross pen and pencil sets seemed to be the most effective with the ladies, and the guys loved a dozen free Titleist golf balls.

My office was in Melrose Park, Illinois a northwest suburb of Chicago. The neighboring town was Cicero, the town where the citizens had been so horrible in their attack on Dr. Martin Luther King Jr., Rev. Jesse Jackson, and the other civil rights marchers when they came through in 1966. I was only 8 years old but I remember how the news reports on television showed a group of maybe a couple of hundred demonstrators being surrounded by a mob of five thousand or more. There were men, women, and children carrying "white power" symbols, cursing and taunting, throwing bottles, bricks, and firecrackers.

Even though the marchers had a police escort, more than half were injured. Dr. King commented that the mobs in that area were more hate-filled and hostile than he had seen in Mississippi and Alabama. I remember Rosie saying to Walter that day as we watched the evening news program on television, "I can't understand how first-and-second generation European immigrants can have so much hate for folks that were here before most of them even got here! I can see a race riot coming; Colored people are not going to stand for this mess."

Rosie's prediction was correct, two days later riots broke out between black residents and police that continued for three or four days. In the end two people, African Americans had been killed and over sixty injured. Members of Chicago's youth street gangs, the Vice Lords, Cobras, and Roman Saints had responded with an explosion of violence that took a personal appeal from Dr. King to their leaders for peace. He had actually called the violent young leaders to the apartment where he was staying and convinced them to halt any further attacks.

Nearly twenty years had gone by since those events. African Americans in Chicago had progressed and efforts had been made to end discrimination. There were open housing laws that had passed, desegregation of public schools, and the establishment of various review boards to control everything from red lining by realtors to police brutality. African Americans had entrenched themselves in the Democratic machine that had been run by Mayor Richard Daley and there was an African American with a realistic possibility of winning the mayor's office in the upcoming election named Harold Washington.

Still I was just a bit nervous about working in the northwest suburbs. There was the issue of being stopped by police in the route from the expressway to the office building that required I drive through a residential area. After all I was a young black man with a fancy car in a neighborhood where blacks didn't live. I concluded that if I drove the speed limit I should be ok since I would always be dressed in a business suit, shirt, and necktie. I found myself so busy and focused on being successful at my work and the rest of life that I didn't have time to worry about it.

My weekly routine included a full day at the office on Mondays to complete paper work associated with the prior week's activities and to make phone calls for scheduling the current week's itinerary. Three days were spent on the road traveling to accounts in Illinois, Iowa, Wisconsin and Indiana. Friday morning in the office, and Friday afternoon on the golf course during warm weather, or in the Loop doing late lunch during winter. This enabled me to get an early start home to beat rush hour traffic. One of our fringe benefits included an AT&T Calling Card, which allowed us to make long distance calls from any telephone. On days that I got home a bit early, I would make business related telephone calls. Most often those phone calls were to collect past due payments or track shipments from the plants.

It was one such Friday evening that I had decided to leave the apartment and travel the short distance to visit Rosie and Walter. I also planned to watch a ball game with frat brothers and friends from the old neighborhood so I stopped at a White Hen Pantry convenience shop at the Hammond, Indiana exit off the expressway to purchase some soda pop, beer, and chips to take along. While in the shop, I spotted a beautiful young woman that I had made the acquaintance of a week or so earlier. One of the friends that I would be watching the game with had taken me along with him to a meeting of the Northwest Indiana Chapter of Black Social Workers. After I arrived I understood why he was an active member. He was the only male; all the other members were attractive young women. I remembered her because I had found her to be the most attractive in the group and had inquired about her in particular with my friend. He said that he didn't know much about her; she was quiet and stayed to herself mostly. He knew that she was single and probably my type since in his opinion she was a bit snobbish. He and I eventually left the meeting before it had completely ended, so she and I didn't get a chance to talk other than to say hello.

In the shop I walked over to her smiled and said, "Hi, I know this sounds like a pickup line, but don't I know you from somewhere? Remember at the Black Social Workers meeting a couple of weeks ago, I came in with my frat brother." She smiled widely and said, "Yeah that's right, I remember. And you're right it does sound like a line." We both chuckled and exchanged names. "Well I'm Barbara, Barbara Felder," she said extending her right hand. "I'm Marsialle Arbuckle, how are you?" I asked while taking her hand into my left hand and stepping closer to her rather that shaking with my right hand. I then glared directly into her eyes for a moment and smiled. Within an instant I could tell that the 'ole emerald greens eyes were doing their trick and having the intended effect. A bit mesmerized, she slanted her head slightly to the right, as she was taken aback from my body language, but smiled widely and said, "I'm fine." Perfect, I thought she was hooked; I was ready to pounce. "Yes you are fine," I said, as I attempted to use my dreamiest, coolest, and most romantic voice. At that point a pretty young girl walked up and said hi. I looked down at her; she looked to be a 13 or 14-year-old model of Barbara. I immediately concluded that the girl must be her younger sibling, so I looked at Barbara and said, "Oh, this is your little sister, huh?" Barbara's eyes lifted with what I know now to be astonishment and said with near laughter in her voice "Yeah she's my little sister." The youngster was about to say something but Barbara cut her off. "Hey go over there and pick out some chips, cookies, and candy bars that you want, I'll be over there in a minute." The youngster walked away shaking her head and mumbling to herself. Hum, I thought to myself, Barbara must have another boyfriend that her sister was about to mention, and she didn't want me to know. That's a good sign, I continued to think, she wants me, yes, she wants me bad.

We went on with a brief conversation, the pleasantries and basics. I finally handed her one of my business cards and said, "If you want to have dinner with a really nice guy that I know give me a call," and began to walk away. She called out to me and said, "Hey, who's the nice guy?" "Me," I answered and we both laughed. The following Tuesday, Barbara called and we planned dinner for the upcoming Friday night, I was to pick her up at 6:30 p.m. sharp, and I promised to be on time.

As you can imagine, I blew it as far as being on time for our first date. As things turned out, Barbara ended up driving to my place and meeting me there. We did have a great date that evening and began to see each other regularly. It was extra convenient to see Barbara almost daily since as it turned out, she lived three blocks from Rosie and Walter. While often my midweek travel would involve an overnight stay, any evening that I was in town included a visit first to them and then Barbara. By the way; the young lady with Barbara in the shop was not her sister, she was our daughter Jamillah. I was correct about one thing, Jamillah was 13 years old.

Chapter 15

As I walked in the door of 2240 Arthur Street one evening late that summer, I was shocked to hear from Rosie that Roland Massie had been by the house just prior to my arrival looking for me. He had left his mother's telephone number and asked that I call him there if I visited that evening. Roland was a tall handsome Black man. He had been very popular with the ladies for as long as I could remember. They liked him for his charming and comedic personality as much if not more than for his good looks. Roland was about 5 years older than I. He had married his college sweetheart Gene and they lived in Lafayette, Indiana. He was an officer in the U.S. Army Reserve and a traveling salesman for a small jewelry design company. Rosie said that Roland really wanted to get in touch with me and said that it was important, so I called him.

He told me that he was traveling to Milwaukee, Wisconsin on the day after the next and wanted to know if we could get together tomorrow evening. Roland said he needed to be in Milwaukee really early and if he could spend the next night at my place it would help him because he could avoid the traffic jam out of Indiana. I said ok and we agreed to meet on the next evening at Sweet Georgia Brown's Lounge on the South Side of Chicago. From there we could go get something to eat and go to my apartment.

The next evening we met according to plan. We downed a couple of beers and chewed the fat. We decided to head out not too long after that since we both had early starts in the morning. Roland really wanted to have White Castle hamburgers for dinner. That wasn't my idea of a good meal but I said what the heck and we went there. He must have eaten 10 or 12 of the little "sliders"; he really enjoyed them and seemed to savor every bite. Once at the apartment Roland and I reminisced about our childhoods and days at West Side C.M.E. Church. We talked about college and our fraternity pledge experience. I noticed that Roland seemed obsessed with security. He checked the locks on the door and the window several times and eventually showed me a small pistol that he planned to sleep with under his pillow. He told me that he had been doing so for the last few weeks. It was as if he was paranoid and that he felt someone was out to get him. I shrugged it off thinking of the crime and violence that I listened to being reported daily and was somewhat understanding of a person having fear of it.

Now I realize that there was no lock or weapon that could have shielded Roland from his predator. Two days later I received a call from Rosie at my office. She told me that Roland had fallen dead while on the dance floor of a club in Milwaukee the night before. Ultimately it was determined that Roland had experienced a massive heart attack. I'm not sure if I was a blessing to Roland and if I provided any comfort beyond camaraderie the night before he died. I do believe that I was a blessing to his mother, sister, wife and brother. I was able to share with them what he had been doing, thinking, and saying that night. I was the last person that they knew personally that had seen Roland alive. They needed me to share with them what happened during the time I spent with someone that they loved so dearly and who left them so unexpectedly. I can never forget the deep despair that his wife Gene was experiencing. Being a blessing isn't easy.

My relationship with Barbara continued to develop. We really seemed to like the same things so dating and our courtship was lots of fun. Barbara, a rather petite woman at about 5 foot 4 inches tall, and a size 4 or 6 six dress had all the right bumps, bulges, and curves. Her light tan brown complexion along with, almond shaped eyes, high cheek bones and a dazzling smile with absolutely perfect teeth makes her ever so pleasant to look at. Her kind, tender and affectionate state of being makes her ever so pleasant to be around.

Barbara is from a large family; she is the oldest of six. She had worked her way through St. Josephs College. She had been married for a short period of time and now was raising Jamillah via joint custody with her ex-husband. Barbara is articulate and has all the social graces, so I would ask her to be my escort on entertainment outings with business associates, which often was a couple's event. Usually this involved attending a professional sports event, going to the theater, opera, or ballet and then dinner at an upscale restaurant in downtown Chicago. It was important that my date not say the wrong thing or conduct herself in an embarrassing fashion and Barbara was sure not to do so. She also had the quick wit to handle sarcastic remarks from any customer that had too much to drink or was just a bonehead. She also knew how to avoid the hot button topics that can turn a pleasant evening into a tense experience that all involved can't wait to be over, religion and politics.

Barbara's father was very well known and prominent in Gary, Indiana. He was a bailiff for the city court, a Precinct Committeeman in his community, and operated a real estate firm, which was his primary focus. Barbara, while a social worker with the Indiana Department of Social Work in the food stamp division, also had a real estate license and worked for her father on the weekends to earn extra money. Since I had saved enough money to afford it and real estate was a sound investment I informed Barbara that I wanted to purchase some real estate and I wanted her to be my agent. She happily agreed saying that she could use the extra money from the commission on the sell.

We began our search for the right investment by looking at duplexes and four or six unit apartment buildings. The idea being that I would live in one of the units and rent the remaining units. That way the building would pay for itself and I could live rent-free and reinvest the savings. It was a sound plan and we worked hard to execute. During the long drives to various potential sites, I began to share my background as well as my long-term dreams, hopes and aspirations with Barbara. I told her about my desire to eventually marry, have children, and live in a big house by the side of the road. I shared with her how I wanted to be well known and prominent like her father and to serve the community and to give back. That I wanted to help foster children in particular because I knew what it was really like and I wanted to do something that might make life just a little bit easier for them. Barbara is a great listener, and being a social worker she is very skilled in the art of "pulling out" what you really feel. She may have used just a wee bit of those skills, as we would talk, because I really opened up to her. I felt that she was really listening carefully and relating totally to what I was saying. I was correct about one thing, she was listening very carefully.

We found a place in Griffith, Indiana that would have been perfect for the investment, but now I was having second thoughts. I was thinking that I might want to ask Barbara to marry me. I knew if I did she'd say yes. I didn't know if the investment approach was wise anymore. I would need that money to buy a home for our family and the building may be difficult to sell. I had to somehow ask her if she thought I should move forward with the approach or buy a house for us, without asking to get hitched yet.

Finally I decided to start dropping hints but not really outright asking, you know the classic beat around the bush. One evening while sitting in her apartment I asked, "Barbara being a real estate agent I'm sure you have your dream house picked out somewhere don't you?" "I sure do," she replied. "It's a place over near Horace Mann High School." "Well, let's go take a look at it," I shot back quickly. The house was beautiful, a two story brick English Tudor style house with large hedges surrounding it. Built in the late 1950's it appeared as a stately manor. We later discovered it had been constructed on behalf of the city police chief at the time. Barbara informed me that the couple that currently lived there was splitting up. They were both long time friends of her father and he was handling the disposal of the property for them. Barbara was shocked when I informed her that it was that house that I wanted to purchase and requested that she arrange the deal. I was shocked when her father attended the closing rather than her. I later discovered that he had to be there because he was the real estate broker; she couldn't be there because she had to be at work at the food stamp office.

There was to be a five-month lag between my closing on the house in late April and moving in the first of October. That would work out great for me since my lease on the apartment in Palos Hills didn't conclude until the end of June. From then I could be on a month-to-month lease, and move out with a 30-day notice to the apartment manager. I had decided that I would ask Barbara to marry me on Mother's Day. That seemed like an appropriate day to make things official. I figured Barbara knew I was going to ask after I purchased the house and was just waiting for me to ask, and probably was wondering what I was waiting for. I didn't want to seem like a guy who was afraid of commitment or couldn't make up his mind about things. That was important especially after I had changed my mind about buying the apartment building. So I purchased diamond studded matching his and her wedding bands, no need to waste money on an engagement ring I thought, and prepared to tell Barbara that I would marry her. My arrogance and ego made me feel as if I were becoming her knight in shining armor and rescuing her from the poverty and despair of single motherhood. At this point I wish books had sound effects because screeching tires would be so appropriate to bring a halt to my ridiculous male chauvinistic thinking. Let us remember that Barbara is a college-degreed, gainfully employed professional whose ex-husband was and is very much involved in the life of his daughter.

That Sunday after arriving back at Rosie's I decided to inform her that Barbara and I would be getting married. She thought it was a great idea. She liked Barbara and thought that she was a classy lady and the type of woman that would be a good wife to a man who "was somebody." Rosie then said what I thought was funny at the time. "Are you sure she wants to marry," she asked. "I know when I was a young woman working a good job and had my own place like that, I sure didn't want to be bothered with a man trying to come lay up on my good living." "Lay up on her!" I exclaimed. "I'll remind you that I make a pretty good living and I'm sure I earn more than she does, besides, you married Daddy." "And I'll remind you that I married him while he was home on leave from the war, there were odds I'd be getting a government bereavement check instead of something to cook and clean for." We both burst into laughter as Rosie pulled a finger up to her lips and gave me the quite sign and a shhh.

I knocked on Barbara's door knowing that she would be home and alone. Since it was the weekend, Jamillah would be at her father's and Sunday afternoons were Barbara's time to do her nails, and other girlie stuff. As I approached her door I could hear music drifting through. It was Luther Vandross, cool I thought, the perfect mood setting music. Barbara opened the door and greeted me with the usual hug and kiss. I sat on the sofa and she sat next to me, I could smell the scent of nail polish remover in the air and the various bottles of beauty supplies were on the coffee table. I decided to be direct and get down to business and that I wasn't going to beat around the bush with this. "Barbara, I'd like for us to get married," I said as I reached in my pocket and presented the ring. It was obvious that she was shocked and stunned. What I then mistook as a level of glee and delight so great that she couldn't speak was actually astonishment and a loss for words. "Well what do you think?" I asked. "They're beautiful," Barbara responded as she stared at the diamonds in the ring. I took that response as a yes since that was all I wanted to hear anyway. "Look baby, I've got to run. I need to stop and tell Mommy and then I've got a tee time. I'll call you tonight." With that I stood pulling her up with me. I gave her a deep and passionate kiss and then headed out the door.

I followed my planned itinerary for the remainder of the day as intended. I gave the news to Rosie and Walter, and shared my good fortune with any and everyone I encountered. After all, I had waited 29 years and this was a big deal. That evening when I approached the door of my apartment I could hear the telephone ringing. I rushed in and grabbed the ringing phone. "Hello Marsialle," it was Barbara, "We need to talk, can I come over?" "Of course, what is it?" I asked. "I need to tell you face to face, I'll see you in about 45 minutes." I showered and prepared something for myself to eat as I waited for Barbara to arrive. I was thinking that Jamillah must have reacted negatively to the news and she wanted to develop a joint strategy on the approach that we would use to deal with the issue. There was a light tap on the door, as I opened it Barbara stood there looking very calm and collected. Whatever the issue was, it was apparent that she had identified the method that would be used to resolve it.

Barbara walked in after my hug and kisses at the door and sat at the dining table rather than on the sofa as usual. She folded her hands and crossed her legs leaned forward and looked directly at me. As she began to speak her tone was professional and matter of fact, "Marsialle, I don't think that it would be a good idea for us to get married." Her words were like a blow to the gut, just below the beltline. My smile shifted to a look of shock, and I pulled out a chair from the table and had a seat. Barbara went on to explain that while she loved me and liked being with me, she had never planned to remarry. She liked her freedom and independence. It had been a struggle to establish herself after her divorce at such a young age and she enjoyed the self-reliance that she had created for herself and her daughter. There was something that she felt was even more important, she had listened carefully to me as I had shared my dreams for the future with her as I had thought. One of the things that caught her attention and became a central point of focus was my desire to have children. Something that was impossible for her to do. She explained that she had been pregnant a second time prior to her divorce but had miscarried. The doctor had informed her that scar tissue had formed and would cause difficulty in childbirth in the unlikely event that she would ever be able to conceive. She knew how much I wanted a family and she did not want to become a lifelong disappointment.

I was shocked, not in my wildest dreams could I have ever imagined that we would find ourselves in this situation and dealing with this set of circumstances. My ego and arrogance had once again clouded my vision and I had not seen what was right before my eyes. As Barbara stood to leave, I asked her not to make a hasty decision. I said that we could figure something out. That there were alternatives like adoption or foster child guardianship. I told her that I loved her and that I wanted to spend the rest of my life with her no matter what. At my urging she put on the ring, and I put on mine. I said that those rings symbolized our union as one and that we would make it.

The following day Barbara had to be out of town for two weeks. As the old saying goes, absence makes the heart grow fonder. When she returned I had a new proposal that we both agreed to, we would simply live together and see how things worked out. If things went well we could adopt or something, and if things didn't go well there wouldn't be the casualty of children. There were two conditions associated with our decision. Barbara was very concerned about the impact that our decision would have on Jamillah. Her daughter would be a freshman in high school that year and she was at a very impressionable age. Barbara did not want to up-root her daughter to move in with me and then have to up-root her again if things didn't work out between us. Therefore I agreed that they could live in the house until after Jamillah's high school graduation, the next four years, regardless of the status of the relationship between Barbara and me. The house was large and if our relationship went sour, we could live on different floors of the house and not interface. We both agreed that in the event that one or the other of us starting seeing someone else, we would respect our home and not have others calling or visiting. The second condition was mine; we would visit an OB-GYN together and get a second opinion about her ability to have children. We did, and the doctor confirmed the first opinion but did say that there was a slight possibility of conception if we used fertility pills. Barbara and I both rejected that idea.

October seemed to roll around quickly and before I knew it our move in date had arrived. I could tell Barbara was extremely apprehensive but love will give courage to the meek and strength to the weak. So we loaded up their things and moved in. Our first night there we had problems. First, Jamillah went into the upstairs bathroom to shower, when the water began running we noticed that it was leaking down into the wall and ultimately came into the ceiling of the kitchen on the floor beneath and leaked down through the light fixture. The previous owners had installed black shag carpeting in the master bedroom. Apparently it somehow had gotten wet and was emitting a foul musty odor. The next morning Barbara got nauseated and had a sort of morning sickness, which continued daily, a result I thought of having to spend the night enduring the smell. I was correct about one thing, Barbara did have morning sickness.

That's right, we were pregnant. The pride and happiness I felt was indescribable. The doctor was shocked when he remembered that he had never written the prescription for the fertility pills. This miracle could only be attributed to God. In the midst of this joy, a terrible tragedy occurred, while out gardening, Rosie had gotten tangled in the water hose and had fallen, the result a broken hip.

Chapter 16

Rosie had been taken to St. Catherine's Hospital in East Chicago, Indiana. I arrived to find Walter in the surgery waiting area. He spoke first, "Would you go in there and see that nurse woman so she can fill out the papers?" Walter was a non-emotional person but this time he was visibly shaken. The look of fear and anxiety was very apparent not only in his voice but also on his face. "How's Mommy?" I inquired. "Not to good," he replied shifting his eyes to the floor. "They need to operate on her but they can't because her heart is too weak and her blood pressure is too high. I think that they're just going to dope her up for awhile until they can get control of her blood pressure." "Ok," I said and headed off to handle the admittance and insurance paperwork.

The next four months were brutal. Not only were they emotionally draining but physically taxing as well. Rosie was a breast cancer survivor and had a serious heart condition. With her advanced age, it had taken the doctors two and a half weeks to stabilize her to a point where they felt she could withstand invasive surgery. She was heavily sedated the entire time. Rosie remained hospitalized for another three weeks after the surgery. Each day I would get up, drop Jamillah off at school, and then go by and visit Rosie until after her breakfast, when Walter would arrive. From there it was off to work. If I wasn't doing an overnighter, I would pick up Jamillah from school, drop her off at home and check the mail while grabbing a sandwich and wait the fifteen to thirty minutes for Barbara to arrive home from work. I would then dash off to the hospital where I would remain until visiting hours ended at 9:30 p.m.

Rosie's recovery and rehabilitation was slow and also brief. She returned home the week of Thanksgiving. Barbara helped me to prepare dinner for Rosie and Walter in their kitchen as well as preparing a full Thanksgiving dinner at our house because her brothers and sisters were coming to visit. Barbara never complained about the double duty or lack of attention and focus on her and our new home and family. Instead she stood in support and provided the stability that held our union together.

"Marsialle, I want something special for Christmas," Rosie was just completing her in-home physical therapy. This entailed her walking from the bedroom, up the hallway to the living room window at exactly 7:45 a.m. each morning. She would then watch the school children making their way to Banneker Elementary School at the end of the block. Her recovery was progressing better than expected, especially considering her age and all of her pre-existing medical conditions. "What's that Mommy?" I inquired. My routine had shifted to stopping by each morning before going to work and assisting with getting her up and going. Her niece from Chicago had come to stay and help with things. Barbara had taken on the task of school drop-off and pickup.

"Well I want two things really. First I want a white suit. I real pretty and fancy one. I want a suit made from silk, like the ones that your wife wears. I want a real nice one from Rosa Lee, or Carson Pirie Scott at the mall. The other thing is I want to have Christmas dinner and invite over Rev. and Sister Jefferson. I want you and Barbara and Jamillah to come too. I need you and Barbara to help me cook and serve and everything. But, I'm going to do most of the cooking. I can sit down and do a lot of stuff."

Rosie's request was fulfilled. Barbara helped me to select the white suit; we also included the accessories, hat, handbag, and gloves. Rosie loved it and proclaimed that it would be her outfit to wear in her triumphant return to church after such a long absence. Her plan was to attend the first Sunday in the year. The dinner was excellent, and Rosie did all of the cooking. When Barbara and I arrived, all that was necessary for us to do was set the table, and place the food into serving dishes for the table. Rosie really appeared to have a grand time. The Rev. John L. Jefferson and his wife Eleanor had been friends of Rosie and Walter since their first days in Gary, Indiana. They came by the house for a visit each Sunday evening. Rosie would set out the good china dishes and real silverware and serve desert and coffee. They would spend the evening talking and enjoying each other's company. It is the result of those visits that I learned the fine art of conversation, wisdom from the wise, and a true sense of Christian fellowship.

Rosie did not get an opportunity to wear her new white suit to attend church. She had a heart attack two days after

Christmas and was returned to the hospital. She remained there until mid-February. Her return to Arthur Street was for a brief two or three days until hospice care could be arranged for her at a hospital in Gary, which was two blocks from my home. It was there that Rosie's transition occurred on February 29th, a day that doesn't occur but once each four years. During Rosie's final days I spent hours and hours at her bedside. Much of that time I spent reflecting on the 28 of my 30 years of existence that had been spent in the love and care of Rosie, my biggest fan. Her love for me, and commitment to me could not be contested. She demonstrated it time and time again by her willingness to sacrifice things for herself so that I could have the best that she could provide.

On the night of Rosie's death, I spent the evening sitting in her room looking out of the window. I thought of all the time she and I spent together at church. I was her escort to board meetings, evening services and other special events like revivals. I thought of one such event when Mommy's favorite sermon had been preached. The sermon ended with a story that I've retained and retold over the years.

This is a story of three young trees by the side of the road. The imagination allows the mind's eye to see these trees as having the ability to communicate with each other. One says to the others, "When you are fully grown what do you want to become that you may be able to leave a legacy that will last forever?" The first tree replies, "When the ax-man comes for me, I want to be fashioned into a baby's crib. Then I shall be passed from generation to generation and my

legacy shall last forever." The second tree responds next, "When the ax-man comes for me I want to be fashioned into a mighty vessel that will sail across the seven seas, and men shall sail me to unknown shores in great adventures and men shall proclaim that I am the greatest of all sea fairing vessels and my legacy shall last forever." The final tree then makes its wish for the future, "My hope is that the ax-man never comes for me and that I may just continue to grow and spread my branches. I shall be a comfort to weary travelers along this road and men shall tell others to look for me as a resting place, and my legacy shall last forever."

Time passes and the ax-man comes for the first tree and chops it down. When it is milled and passed to the carpenter, rather than being fashioned into a baby's crib, it was made into a manger. It is designed into a manger to be used for the purpose of feeding farm animals in a barn. The manger is then placed in a barn behind a small inn. That inn is located in a town called Bethlehem in Judea. On a cold winters night a young couple could not find a place to stay and they took refuge in the barn. The young woman gave birth to a child that night and they placed him in that manger. That child was Jesus Christ, and that manger remains a part of the nativity display that has been passed down for 2009 years. Things don't happen the way you want them to; remember that God has a plan.

As more time passed the ax-man came for the second tree and chopped it down. After being milled it was taken to a shipyard, but rather than becoming a great sailing ship, it was made into a small cuddy ship destined to sail back and forth across the Sea of Galilee. On a windy and stormy day a band of twelve or so men stepped aboard that small cuddy to cross the Sea of Galilee. As the storm began to rage and the bellows began to roar, a man stepped off the vessel and onto the sea and as he walked upon the water, he calmed the storming sea. That man's name was Jesus Christ and the story of that small vessel is recorded in a book that has been read by more people than any other book of time, the Holy Bible. Things don't happen the way you want them to; remember that God has a plan.

More time passed, and to its' dismay, the ax-man chopped down that third tree that just wanted to grow and grow. When milled the timber was not sanded. It was just cut into two large sections and rushed to the foot of a hill in a location called Mt. Calvary. There the timber was nailed into the shape of a cross and lifted by a man to be dragged to the top of that hill. As he stumbled a second man was forced to help him. At the top of the hill, the first man was nailed to the cross and lifted to hang there until his death. His name was Jesus Christ. Today, some 2009 years later, women and men the world over bring their weary and burdened souls to the foot of the cross to find comfort

and peace. Things don't happen the way you want them to; remember God has a plan.

God's plan for Rosie, Walter, and me was unfolding. Rosie and Walter had been placed in my life to provide aid for me when I wasn't able to do so, and now in His miraculous glory, the Lord had brought me back to them. God wanted me to provide aid for them in their time of need. Walter would need me now almost as much as I needed him twenty eight years ago. His needs would be different; he would need companionship as well as someone to help him with the "paper work" throughout the rest of his life.

The first task in my role as Walter's business manager was to arrange Rosie's memorial service. It was a consuming task but the busy pace kept my mind occupied and therefore not focused on grief. Everything had to be done in one week's time. The mortician made us aware of this during our initial visit when we learned of the costs. It was then that we had to complete the grim task of selecting the casket and determining the number of limousines that would be required for the family procession to the cemetery. Both key factors in establishing the cost; they were also undisputable evidence that Rosie was really gone.

There were relatives from out of town to contact and inform. There were arrangements with the mortuary, florist and church. There was the writing of the obituary, memorial service program, and newspaper notice. There was the contacting of the minister to present the eulogy, and other church members that would participate in the memorial service such as the soloist and organist. There was contacting insurance companies, the

Social Security Administration and the banks. We contacted department stores and credit card companies to close accounts. We had to contact the cemetery to have the date placed on the pre-purchased headstone and the pre-purchased gravesite opened and setup for a burial. There were arrangements made to have Rosie's hair and nails done, and the delivery of her new white silk suit to the mortuary. The suit would now serve as her shroud for her triumphant return to glory.

Somebody had to do all of those things. Those things that everybody expected to be done and somebody had to do them. The telephone seemed to ring constantly. Everything required follow-up and nobody else was the contact person. Somebody had to be in charge, though I didn't want the responsibility because I felt tired, I had to step up because I had made a promise to Rosie to be somebody. It was then that I could understand Rosie's seemingly simple and almost minimal aspiration for my brother and me. Her goal for our future endeavors took on gigantic proportion that would require a lifetime of committed service and ceaseless endeavor. I finally understood the significance of those two words, be somebody. I now knew who somebody is;

> Somebody is the person that does what anybody
> could do, But nobody does it,
> Because everybody knows that,
> Somebody will do it, and I, yes I, am somebody.

I had heard Rosie say it so many times, "I want you to be somebody." I had stood in church on Saturday, after Saturday throughout my youth, and had proclaimed it at the top of my voice, "I am somebody!" I felt in my inner being that it was God's plan for me to be somebody, and I vowed then to commit the remainder of my life to being somebody; the person that does what anybody could do, but nobody does it, because everybody knows that 'ole somebody is going to get the job done. I couldn't let fatigue be the victor.

I remembered a comment that I had made to Frank Pace during our days back at Indiana University. We had been assigned the final shift of collecting admittance fees for a function the fraternity was sponsoring. The function was our annual fundraiser and its success was critical to the financial viability of the chapter. It was late that night, we were tired and we both wanted to enjoy the great event that was happening behind us. Frank looked at me and suggested that we close down our booth, let everyone else in free since it was late, and enjoy the party. Looking at the number of folks in line that were still willing to pay and knowing the financial status of our chapter at the time, I looked at Frank and said firmly, "Now's not the time to get tired, now is the time to get responsible!" Those words seemed to rally Frank and we completed our task. Frank has proclaimed those words as a profound statement that he has remembered and reminded me of on numerous occasions.

It was time for me to rally myself with my own words and follow my own advice. I did and everything was done. The service reflected the honor and dignity that Rosie had incorporated into her daily living. **Ecclesiastes 3:1-2, To everything there is a season and a time to every purpose under the heaven. A time to be born, and a time to die; a time to plant, and a time to pluck up that which is planted.** God's plan had evolved to the point when it was time for Rosie to take off her full gospel armor, her breastplate of righteousness and stick her sword in the sands of time. I knew that she believed in the resurrection of the body and eternal life, and if I believed, then I would see her again on the other shore.

Chapter 17

Over the next few weeks, life seemed to return to normal. My grief faded and my sorrow was overcome by the joy attached to the current events. Once again the truth in the Word of the Holy Bible was revealed, **Psalm 30:5, For his anger endureth but a moment; in his favor is life: weeping may endure for a night, but joy cometh in the morning.** My weeping became joy as a new life sprung forth in the form of my son Marseille, Jr.

On Friday, April 15th, while driving home from my Chicago office, I decided I would ask Barbara to marry me again. I had no reason not to be married to Barbara; the family that I wanted was already in place. The fruit of my loins was expected to arrive in another two or three months and I didn't want that to occur without the proper vows having been exchanged. After all, I didn't want Rosie's memory or my child's good name to be tarnished, parishioners do whisper during the blessing of an infant.

That evening after I humbly ask Barbara to marry me, on one knee and everything, she agreed with one condition, no big ceremony. She felt that those funds could be better utilized for our home and family rather than to wine and dine a group of folks to witness our "I do's." Barbara pointed out that we needed new carpeting and central air conditioning, and those dollars could be used for that. I agreed with her and accepted the condition. The following day we were married in the office of a minister that Barbara had known for several years. Jamillah served as her Maid of Honor, and Thomas Wise was my Best Man.

Two days later on Monday morning I headed off to my office in Melrose Park, Illinois, smug and happy with my new formal and official family. At about 11:45 a.m., just before lunch, I called Barbara at her office. I told her how happy I was that we had gotten married on Saturday and checked with her to see if she was feeling ok. Barbara responded with equal joy over our decision and indicated that she was doing fine. We both said that we would go to lunch and talk at home in the evening.

I left the office and went to lunch at a local restaurant near the office and returned within an hour. When I sat at my desk I noticed a phone message was waiting so I checked it. "Hi Marsialle, it's me Barbara. I was sitting in the drive thru line at Burger King and my water broke. There was a car in front of me and in back of me so I just waited in line, paid for my order at the window and then drove myself to Methodist Hospital. I'll see you there, bye." Needless to say, I erupted into a nervous wreck. I ran to my car, jumped in, turned on the emergency flashers and began speeding toward Indiana. It was midday so traffic was light and I was able to get to the hospital in about 50 minutes, which is record time.

When I arrived in the birthing room, Barbara smiled a half grin, you know the kind someone gives when they're in pain but attempting not to show it. "Hi honey, can you believe this? This isn't supposed to happen for two months," Barbara said with a tone of amusement. "Do you think everything is alright?" I inquired. "Oh yeah, it's just that our little one is a bit impatient that's all. The doctor has been in and checked me out and he thinks that everything is fine. Would you go and park my car for me? I left it in the driveway of the emergency area."

With a sigh of relief I leaned over Barbara, gave her a kiss and headed off to move her car. As I opened the door to the car, I noticed the bag sitting in the front passenger's seat. It contained the fish sandwich and fries that Barbara had ordered for lunch. No need for these to go to waste, I thought to myself. So, I ate them as I moved Barbara's car to the parking lot.

I returned to the birthing room and began to watch my wife suffer through the ordeal of labor. The doctor had been correct in his assessment that childbirth and delivery would be extremely difficult. The following day after 24 hours of suffering, the doctor concluded that our son should be delivered via cesarean section rather than traditionally and Barbara was carried off to surgery. One hour or two later a nurse came to inform me that I had a son and took me around to the premature delivery ward to see my son for the first time.

Marseille was so tiny on that first day of his entry into the world that I could literally hold him in the palm of one hand, and none of his body or limbs would extend beyond my fingertips. He also had a heart murmur, which required the doctors to install an intravenous injection line. Due to his tiny dimensions, the only vein useable was in his forehead. While the doctor said it didn't cause him any pain, little Marseille looked so distressed with that tube running from the middle of his tiny little head. I prayed that God would give my son strength. **Psalm 28:1, Unto thee I cry, O Lord my rock; be not silent to me: lest, if thou be silent to me, I become like them that go down into a pit. Hear the voice of my supplications, when I cry unto thee, when I lift up my hands toward thy holy oracle.**

God answered my prayers, Marseille grew rapidly and his heart developed to be strong and capable. He was able to come home with us within two weeks. I praised God for His mercy and rejoiced in the glory of the truth of the Word of the scriptures. **Psalm 28:6-7, Blessed be the Lord, for he hath heard my supplications. The Lord is my strength and my shield; my heart trusted in him, and I am helped: therefore my heart greatly rejoiceth; and with my song will I praise him.**

Barbara was allowed to come home after one week. She was not able to walk up or down stairs for nearly a month so I and Jamillah made countless trips up and down the stairs, especially after Marseille came home. Fortunately Ford Motor Company had instituted maternity leave for new fathers as well as mothers by 1988. I was allotted two weeks paid leave that I added with two weeks of vacation time, enabling me to spend four weeks helping with the chores and bonding with my new son.

Life got into the routine of an infant in the house, and all the associated tasks. Jamillah was becoming a beautiful young teenager and our mantle was adorned with trophies and certificates that were the rewards of her achievement academically or in track & field, softball, National Honor Society, and varsity cheerleading. We were then blessed with another addition to the family. Jamillah brought Rodney into the world for us all to share and love. Since this book is about me and not anyone else, I won't spend time on the circumstances attached to that situation. Needless to say there was turmoil in the household. The turmoil quickly subsided with Rodney's arrival. He was here, he could not be sent back only loved and nurtured. Rodney made that part easy; he was just an adorable baby. He was always smiling and cooing. This little bundle of joy was oblivious to any controversy or turmoil that his existence may have caused; rather he was just happy to be here with everyone else. They say that timing is everything, and Rodney's timing was perfect. He was born in the summer between school years, and Jamillah never missed one day of high school. She maintained her high scholastic achievement at school and ultimately earned a position of honor in her graduating class, receiving a full four-year academic scholarship to Michigan State University. During that time Jamillah also managed the full responsibility of motherhood and developed a special bond with little Rodney. Of course Barbara and I, along with the extended families all helped.

Chapter 18

My life moved along at a fast pace. Work life and home life seemed to integrate smoothly and with ease. I enjoyed my work and my family. We continued our routines even though hectic most of the time, Barbara and I were able to enjoy going out through entertaining my customers. I was pleasantly surprised to discover that she was a true to life basketball fan with actual knowledge of the history of the game and players along with the rules and statistics. She loved going to the Chicago Bulls games. Barbara, I, and little Marseille would pack up and go. The Ford seats were great, directly behind the Jordan family seats. The customers loved the opportunity to feel like a celebrity and so did we.

While driving to a game one evening I was quietly driving along pondering some thoughts when Barbara asked what was I thinking about? I told her that in honesty, I was thinking that it was absolutely hilarious to me that within two years I had transitioned from a swinging bachelor living alone to a grandfather living with a wife, a teenager, a toddler, and an infant, and began laughing. When I looked over to Barbara she wasn't smiling but looking at me very seriously, so I asked what she was thinking. She said that she was thinking that her respect for me as a man was equal to her love for me. She said that as a social worker she encountered families with serious issues regularly. More than once she had seen issues like ours destroy a home. She had encountered recently a fellow that had told his wife that her pregnant daughter had to leave or he was gone. She said that she was thankful for my acceptance of the situation. I was really choked up, my only response was, "I love you madly, and I always will." I then attempted to croon a bit of "It Feels So Good to Be Loved So Bad," by The Manhattans; I was so off key Barbara burst into laughter.

Shortly after that evening out in Chicago, a tragedy struck that would be so devastating it would rock our entire world. Mr. Felder, Barbara's father died the victim of a horrible violent act. The circumstances involved with the situation impacted us all significantly. Especially Barbara, she seemed to drift into a near state of hypnosis. She functioned daily, performing tasks and even going to work, but it wasn't the same Barbara. I didn't know exactly what to do other than to be there for her, to be understanding and empathetic, and to pray. Once again the truth of the Holy Word was revealed. **Psalm 107:6, Then they cried unto the Lord in their trouble, and he delivered them out of their distresses.** Just as time had absorbed my pain and helped me overcome my grief with Rosie, so to was Barbara able to overcome hers.

As we once again drifted into the fast paced routine we called life, God's plan included many blessings for us. Both Barbara and I were advancing our careers and receiving promotions and pay increases at work. That certainly enhanced our quality of life. I was becoming involved in civic and community activities. I was selected to fill a vacant seat on the Board of Managers of the John Will Anderson Boys & Girls Club. That opportunity was especially important to me because my brother and I had attended the Club and I felt that it was a way to give back. Ford allowed me to use some of my annual promotion budget dollars to cover the cost of sponsorship gifts for the annual golf outing fundraiser each year. I also attended monthly meetings to lend my managerial expertise to the operation of the facility.

I was also active with the fraternity alumni chapter and regularly attended church with active participation. I also requested that Ford allow me to sponsor the local "Night Out Against Crime" event in our community with some of my promotion budget. With Ford Motor Company's financial and management support we hosted the event for six of the eight years that we lived there. It took place each summer in the parking lot of Horace Mann High School that was directly across the street from our home. There would be free ice cream cones, soda pop, hot dogs, and chips. The local Ford dealership would bring over a couple of display vehicles and pass out free tee shirts. There would be a fire engine from the local fire station along with balloons and clowns. One of my fraternity brothers, Indiana State Trooper Tyrone Cox would bring over his state police department squad car and put it on display. The Boys & Girls Club would bring over a busload of kids and they would join in with the kids from the neighborhood for fun and games led by the firemen and parents. All arranged by Barbara and me, with everything donated by folks in our network. That's when I realized the power of networking.

Also and more importantly, I realized the power of God. It was obvious to me that a portion of God's plan for me was service. It was clear that the more I served, the more he empowered me to do so. The more I did for the benefit of and to bless others, the more I was being blessed. But remember being a blessing isn't easy.

In addition to visiting Walter each day, I had added another regular visit to my schedule. Once a week on the way in from the office on Monday evening, I would drop in on Uncle George Arbuckle and his wife Aunt Lillian. They lived in a small brownstone just off the expressway on Chicago's South Side. I actually had to pass right by it on my way home if I used the Skyway that often had the least amount of traffic because it is a toll way. They were getting on in their years, and since they had no children I felt it was my responsibility to check on them. George was actually my Great Uncle in as much as he was actually my Grandfather's younger brother.

Uncle George and I had developed a strong relationship during my teen years. Each summer just prior to the return of school and at the end of our National Youth Corp employment I would visit Uncle George for a long weekend. He would drive over from Chicago and pick me up on Thursday and return me to Gary the following Monday. I started my first NYC job at age 14 and have worked each year of my life since. Uncle George would take me shopping on Maxwell Street in one of Chicago's shopping districts where negotiating, or better said haggling, over the price of an item was a part of the purchase process.

We would eat at restaurants and he would take me to church on Sunday, where he sang in the choir and male chorus.

George was a fairly well educated man. He had completed a two-year business college after returning from the war and was a retired receiving supervisor, from a midsize distribution company. I recall that two of their key products were Woolite laundry soap and Glade air freshener. His wife Lillian was a retired schoolteacher. From my earliest visits to their home I recall Aunt Lillian as a recluse. During my visits she never came out from her bedroom, rather she would speak to me from behind the door. There were only four occasions that I can recall when she left their house. She attended both Michael and my high school graduation ceremonies, a conversation that I had with her on the front porch of their home once when Uncle George was hospitalized, and her funeral. I'm positive that she went out more often, those are the only occasions that I can recall.

George and I had long talks during my visits with him. He had explained that Aunt Lillian began behaving in a strange fashion after a nasty rumor circulated at their church regarding her relationship with another woman member. Aunt Lillian stopped going out, first to church and other places, then she put a television in the bedroom and only came out to eat. It got so bad that he had threatened to institutionalize her if she failed to manage personal hygiene, which had occurred more than once. George said that he had decided early on that he wasn't going to let a rumor impact his life even if she did, so he continued to move forward in his life. I wondered if that was the reason they had not taken us in when we were abandoned. It seemed as if he liked me and I didn't see any reason for him not to have taken us since they had no children of their own. I never asked Uncle George that question.

One question that I did ask is where our last name of Arbuckle comes from. His answer was honest and true, "I don't know for sure but there is as folktale that my grandmother told me. Would you like to hear it?" "Of course," I replied.

The story is set in the late 1700's before the Civil War. It takes place somewhere in the deep woods of southeastern Tennessee. A group of slaves ran away. They were spotted as missing early on and the slave hunters were tracking them and not far off their trail. As time passed the escapees started getting tired and they would drop off and tell the others to keep going. You could hear their screams in the distance as the hounds would attack them and their captors beat and shackled them for return.

It finally got down to one remaining escapee on the run. He was so tired that he couldn't go on either and he fell down and then he crawled to a tree stomp and got on it and sat there. When he looked up he could see that he was sitting in front of a small farmhouse, with a barn on the side. A man who appeared to be the owner was standing there in the yard. That man was a white man, with two big mean and viscous looking dogs, one on each side.

The man motioned for the dogs to attack and they began to run at the escapee, but when they got to

him, he started to pet them and play with them. The old farmer was shocked and scared. Back in those days, if a man did anything considered unusual, he was immediately branded a user of witchcraft. That's exactly what the farmer thought as he watched his dogs playing with the man instead of ripping him apart. When the farmer's wife and son came out to see what all the commotion was, the farmer told her his fears and she begged him to ask the warlock what it was that he wanted so they could get him to go away.

To calm his wife the farmer did as she wanted and asked the strange man who he was and what he wanted. Recognizing the situation and knowing his circumstances the man answered the farmer's question with a question, "Tell me your name and that of the boy and I will tell you who I am." The farmer replied, "I'm the owner of this property and my son and I are going to run you out of here if you don't tell me what it is that you want. Matthew, go get my shotgun." "Don't move!" the escapee stood and shouted. The boy froze in his spot. Once again recognizing his situation and knowing the circumstances the escapee responded with a question, "Do you want to live in peace, happiness and prosperity?" "Yes," the farmer replied. "Then show me friendship and love and I will tell you the truth." The frightened farmer and his wife along with their son looked at each other and then the farmer replied, "We will show you friendship and love that we may know the truth and live in peace, happiness, and prosperity." The escapee then told them that there were men with guns and animals following him and that they would arrive soon. He told them that they should hide him in the barn and say that they had not seen anything of him and send the men away. He told the farmer and his family, "That act of friendship and love will bring you peace and happiness, and prosperity will soon follow."

Without much time to think the farmer and his family agreed, and hid the escapee in the barn. When the slave hunters arrived at the farm they were told that no one was there except the family and that no one had been seen in that last several days. After the slave hunters were gone the farmer and his wife approached the strange man again and said, "We've shown you an act of friendship and love because you told us the truth. Is there anything else that we must do for peace, happiness and prosperity before you leave?" One again recognizing his situation and knowing the circumstances the escapee replied, "Yes, please allow me to stay here until I've learned to read. During that time I will be your servant and help you plant your fields of corn and wheat. My work is like that of two men. With your son that will yield you three times your normal harvest and you will live in the prosperity that I promised you earlier." The farmer and his wife agreed.

As the bountiful harvest was nearing completion the farmer's wife had nearly completed the task of teaching the escapee to read. She used the Holy Bible as her teaching tool. The escapee began to prepare to leave the farm. On his final day the escapee approached the farmer. He told the farmer that he needed one last bit of help. He needed a name, and he asked the farmer, "May I take on your name as my name?" Recognizing the situation and knowing the circumstances the farmer answered the question with a question, "Do you want to live in peace, happiness and prosperity?" "Yes," the escapee responded with a smile. "Promise me that as an act of friendship and love you will teach others of your kind to read that they may know the truth. If you promise me that, I will give you my name that you may live in peace, happiness, and prosperity." "I promise," said the escapee. "My name is Arbuckle," said the farmer, "Matthew Arbuckle."

Equipped with his new name and $20 he had received from the farmer as his share of the harvest from the crops, M. Arbuckle, as he would call himself, moved on and traveled further into Tennessee and established a homestead near a place now called Martin, Tennessee. The first one room school house for the Colored in that region was run by Mrs. Arbuckle, who had been taught to read by her husband. She was the widow of a farmer that no one knew where he had come from.

On more than one occasion I had asked Uncle George was his story true. He would tell me legend had it that the original farmer Matthew Arbuckle was killed and his farm wiped out by a flood. His son became a military leader during the Civil War and afterwards traveled west to Oklahoma to fight in the Indian battles. During my travels in Oklahoma, I had an opportunity to visit the Arbuckle Mountains and Davis, Oklahoma that was formerly Arbuckle, Oklahoma. Both were named in honor of Brigadier General Matthew Arbuckle that had come from the East and established Fort Arbuckle during the Indian uprisings. I have not researched the matter any further, probably for fear of disproving the authenticity of the legend as much as anything else.

I am a member of the Grand United Order of Odd Fellows. The organization is a religious fraternal order. A dispensation was granted to establish a lodge in America in 1844. Peter Ogden a man of African descent from New York City, New York became a steward on the steamship "Patrick Henry" plying between New York and Liverpool, England. He was initiated in Victoria Lodge No. 448 while there and attained the various degrees of rank within the Order during subsequent visits. In 1842, his ship arrived in New York where he learned of the efforts of a Literary and Social Society attempting to be chartered as a Lodge of the Odd Fellows and how they were denied that privilege by established lodges in New York and Pennsylvania because of their African descent. Peter Ogden offered to negotiate with his Lodge in England to see if they could offer any assistance. As a result of his efforts, Peter Ogden was given the dispensation to charter Lodge No. 646 New York by the Committee of Management in England.

Philomathean Lodge No. 646 is still in existence. The Grand United Order of Odd Fellows now has branches throughout the United States, also in Canada, Liberia, Africa, Cuba, Haiti, Puerto Rico, Dominican Republic, Bermuda, Bahamas, Jamaica, Netherlands, West Indies, Costa Rica, Nicaragua, Virgin Islands, British Honduras, Trinidad, St. Kitts B.W.I., Barbados, and several other islands of the West Indies.

I took the time to share that with you so you could understand my affiliation with the organization beyond its motto and the motto of the women's auxiliary, The Household of Ruth. The motto's are Friendship, Love, and Truth; Peace, Happiness, and Prosperity respectively. Over the years I been an active member and served as an international officer on the Committee of Management of America and Jurisdiction. I am currently the Director of Area III that includes Michigan, Illinois, Indiana, Wisconsin, and Kentucky. Marseille, Jr. and Rodney are members and serve as Michigan District Officers. Both Barbara and Jamillah are members of the Household of Ruth. It is my desire that we pass the legacy of the Order on to future generations. It is apparent to me that my Great-Great Grandmother had woven the principles of the Order and the Household into the story that she told to George even if she was a member or not.

On one of my visits to Uncle George he informed me the he would need to do a three day stay in the hospital for tests. He asked that I stop over and check in on Aunt Lillian. He gave me a key to the door and said that when I enter the house, just call out to her and she would respond from behind the bedroom door as usual. If she didn't respond there may be a problem, so I should enter the room and check things out because she had been feeling very poorly but had refused to leave the house to go for a checkup. He said I only needed to check on the second day, she would be fine for the first day and he would be back during the afternoon of the third day. I agreed and the following week I arranged my schedule so I could stop in as promised. When I arrived Aunt Lillian was sitting in a chair in the living room.

To say that I was shocked would be an understatement. I had not actually seen Aunt Lillian in almost 8 or 9 years, not since high school graduation. She was wearing a blue flowered print duster. Her hair was gray and long but uncombed. It was matted in the back showing the hours of laying her head on the pillow. While her complexion was a coffee with light cream brown, she almost appeared gray, the tone of her skin flat and dry looking. Her fingernails were long dark brown spirals that curled under. She was smiling, her teeth were bright white but long and disarranged. "Hi Marsialle, I've been expecting you, George told me you would stop by around this time." "Hi Aunt Lillian," I replied attempting to conceal my amazement at both her being there and her appearance. "Is everything ok, are you doing alright?" "Oh, yes I'm doing fine. I just got done eating a little something that I fixed for myself. Have you talked to George today?" Her voice sounded strong and clear, as she stood and shuffled toward me. No, I've been at work all day and I just stopped in to check on you," I replied. We continued to chat for a few minutes, nothing profound, just the weather and traffic were our topic. Then another unusual event occurred, as I walked out of the door, Aunt Lillian followed me out onto the front porch. The woman that had always spoken to me from behind a door was now standing outside of the house.

She turned her face to the sun, closed her eyes and took a deep breath as if to soak it in. I don't recall exactly what it was that we chatted about, but I do remember we stood and talked for a while, maybe ten or so minutes before I left. When I reported the incident to Uncle George the next day he was shocked. Two weeks later Uncle George called me to inform me that Aunt Lillian had passed away the night before, quietly in her sleep.

I'm not sure if I was a blessing to Aunt Lillian during our brief discussion, but I am sure that I was a blessing for Uncle George during his time of loss. I stood at his side, at the mortuary as he made memorial arrangements. I went with him into the room at the funeral parlor to select the casket and shroud. I helped him make telephone calls to friends, the cemetery, and the church. I helped him make arrangements with a beautician, musician, and florist. I helped him write the death notice for the local newspaper, and develop the memorial service program for printing. I rode with him in the limousine to the church, cemetery, and back home on the day of the funeral. I helped him mourn his late wife of over forty years. Being a blessing isn't easy.

Chapter 19

At the turn of the summer season that year, my brother Michael was promoted to the position of Revenue Officer for the Internal Revenue Service. He was relocated to the South Bend, Indiana office, and he decided to live in Gary since it was only a thirty-minute drive and often his assignments were for locations in the Chicago area. Michael's alternative and main purpose for living in Gary was to be closely located to his childhood pals that were still living in town. He knew that to find the 'ole gang only involved a stop at the old hang out, the parking lot of LRC Liquor Store on the corner of 21st Avenue and Grant Street.

LRC, was the late nightspot place to be. It was almost a rite of passage for the young men in our neighborhood, or the hood as we called it, to hang-out there. Everyone had a nickname; Lefty, Chico, B.T., Poochie, Naked, Huey P., Stoney, Bobo, Pookie, Big Nasty, June-Bug, Buck, and Tiny just to name a few. I must admit that it was there that I learned what is commonly referred to as "street smarts." Many brave talking guys had been humbled and embarrassed when put in a position to backup his talk. Knowing when to fight or back-down is a part of the street smarts that can only be developed in real life situations. All kinds of "stuff" happened at LRC, deals were made, items fenced, drugs sold, bets placed, and just about any type of vice imaginable took place in the lot. You were respected if you got involved in "stuff" and were successful, and equally respected if you displayed the self-confidence and self-discipline to avoid involvement. If you came from the hood and you wanted to be respected, you just about had to hang at LRC at some time or another.

The building had two sections, in the front there was the liquor store, and the back half of the building was a carry out Bar-B-Q restaurant. The ribs were great, but the sauce was a bit lacking, however, after a couple of beers everything tasted good. The lot would be crowded with patrons of the store and restaurant. The fellas would hang out in the back half of the lot, standing around the one or two cars that belonged to someone from the hood. As young men right out of high school, U.S. Steel employed many of the guys. They would immediately purchase a brand new car and show it off in the lot. I was often ridiculed for going to college and being broke, rather than taking a job at the "big mill," as it was called, and making some money. After the economic downturn of the late 1970's U.S. Steel reduced its work force at the Gary mill from almost 20,000 employees to just over 5,000. Those with the least seniority were the first to be let go. Of course that included the fellas from the hood; so many of them were unemployed, under educated and unhappy.

Michael was welcomed with open arms by the 'ole gang. He wasn't aware that the culture of the corner and the behavior of its inhabitants had changed. It was the same people but with a totally new set of issues and values. The old code of "One for all and all for one," had shifted to a new code, "You know how we do," which really meant, "I don't have anything to offer but since you know me, let me have yours, and if you don't give it to me, I'll take it." People that he considered friends were really parasites that wanted to suck him financially dry. The factor that caused the shift in values and culture was not directly job loss, but the result of it. Unemployment and everything associated with it causes a lack of self-esteem and unhappiness that can lead to depression. When an individual realizes they aren't equipped to change the situation because of insufficient skills and education, then one loses hope which causes deeper depression. To combat depression, many chose to self-medicate, and the available drug of choice was crack cocaine.

At first I didn't notice that Michael had changed. He would stop by the house on a regular basis, often grabbing a bite to eat. Since he was a bachelor, I accounted it to his wanting some home cooking rather any money woes that he may be having. Then his visits became knocks on the door late at night wanting to borrow some money. He would say that he had been drinking or hanging out and that his cash was low. He would say that he had an early appointment and ask for twenty or thirty dollars to cover gas and lunch for the next day. After eight or nine times, I knew there was a problem. It didn't take much investigation to discover that Michael had developed an addiction.

I had no idea of the far-reaching effects and impact of crack cocaine. I knew that it was an addictive drug similar to heroine, but I didn't have a clue as to the power it has to take control of a person's mind. The discoveries that I would make as I stepped into the world of crack to save my brother would shock and amaze me, as well as, disgust and sicken me. People that I least expected to be users were, and the means that they would go to in order to obtain the drug and support their habit was astounding. It reached across all boundaries, including age, gender, race, ethnicity, religion, education, and socio-economic status.

My first confrontation with Michael regarding crack came after he had been fighting and threatened at LRC by one of the gang. He came to the house with blood running down his face and neck from a head wound. He said that he owed money to the person and when he didn't have it, the person attacked him unexpectedly and caught him by surprise. When I asked Michael how much and who, I became irate as I discovered the amount was $8 and the person was someone we had known all our lives. I became so filled with rage that I grabbed a small handgun that I owned and took Michael in my car back to the scene with the full intention of confrontation. As we turned into the lot, the culprit spotted us and ran off through a small wooded area behind the lot. I jumped from the car and began to chase the person. After a few yards I stumbled and then stopped. I asked myself what I would do if I caught the person. The answer was not good, and I thank God that he was my stumbling block and that he touched me and brought me back to my senses. I walked back to the car and sat down. By that time a crowd had gathered, wanting to know what was next.

When I returned home the impact of the incident took full effect. I started to think about all of the horrible things that could have resulted. I thought of my wife and son and how terrible things would be for them if something had happened. I looked at myself in the mirror and promised to never again let myself drift into the same level of irrational behavior. I also thought of the irony of the situation. Michael had been my defender and protector all of our lives. It was always Michael that took the blame. It was always Michael that went first. It was Michael that had walked me to school and fought off the bullies at the Boys Club and YMCA.

Michael had begun playing football at Beckman Middle School in 9th grade. By his senior year in high school he had developed the physique of an athlete and he had the toughness to go with it. After a year of college he enlisted in the Marines to support his newly created family that included a wife and my nephew Michael, Jr. and niece Nicole. After being honorably discharged from military service Michael and his wife were divorced. He started playing semi-pro football with a team in Indianapolis to take a new direction in life. When his pro tryouts weren't successful Michael completed his college degree and began working for the Internal Revenue Service. Now our roles of big brother protecting his little brother were reversed all because of this new drug.

Crack cocaine had begun to take hold of our entire community. The cost of crack cocaine and accessibility along with its euphoric and addictive affect made it the new oppressor of our people. The most shocking element of its affect was its powerful mind control. It has the ability to make a person no longer care about the impression they make or impact their actions have on others or themselves. With total disregard for impression or impact, individuals do the unthinkable. There is no need to detail the next few months other than to say it drove us to seek professional assistance in order to address the matter. More importantly we turned to the ultimate power, we prayed. I'm happy to report that Michael has overcome his addiction and enjoys a happy and productive life. Once again the truth of the Holy Word was revealed; **Isaiah 25:8-9, He will swallow up death in victory; and the Lord God will wipe away tears from off all faces: and the rebuke of his people shall he take away from off all the earth: for the Lord hath spoken it. And it shall be said in that day, Lo, this is our God; we have waited for him, and he will save us; this is the Lord; we have waited for him, we will be glad and rejoice in his salvation.**

Chapter 20

On November 8, 1992, I received word that Augustine Arbuckle had passed away. Four years after Rosie had been buried, I found myself in the position to bury my mother for a second time. Death was something that I was becoming too familiar with, and now I was facing round two of the agony of losing Augustine for a second time. She had left us once before, but with a promise to return, a promise that I didn't understand because I was too young to comprehend; Michael didn't understand the promise because he was too young to know it wasn't true; Montclair didn't understand the promise because he knew it wasn't true. That lack of understanding significantly impacted the rest of each of our lives, especially our perception of the reality of life in a foster home. I had the ability to totally bond with my foster mother and father and totally accept them as my parents. Michael was just old enough to know, and he adapted rather than to bond. Adapting rather than bonding may seem like a subtle difference, but it was really major in his perception of the world, and we know that perception is reality.

Michael looked at things just a bit differently than I did. A spanking in his opinion was, "People hitting him who had no business doing so, because they weren't his momma or daddy." He would console himself with the thought that "My real mommy and daddy are going to come and rescue me someday, because mommy promised." That thought process can become a tremendous burden and source of deep psychological stress on an individual. Imagine crying yourself to sleep with that thought on a regular basis, which Michael did. Remember, Rosie was a strict disciplinarian so a spanking before bed was a regular occurrence.

While there is no doubt or question that Michael loved both Rosie and Walter, and they loved him, and they all knew that they loved each other, Michael never lost or overcame the natural and instinctive desire to be with his biological parents. While I have no professional training for my opinion, and can only support it with the "I lived it" degree, from the school of experience, I believe that "the promise" was the root cause of Michael's "self-medication" issues.

While I bonded, and Michael adapted, Montclair did neither. Rather, he decided to fight the power. Montclair had a totally different experience with the foster care system. He saw the ugly side of the program, being abused because of his difficult behavior and being transferred from home to home as he was rejected by foster parents that couldn't "control" him. Montclair had totally understood "the promise" and knew that it wasn't true. He had been abused and mistreated by not only Augustine and Willie, but their drug using friends when they were around as well. Adults had wronged him, he didn't trust them, and he wasn't going to allow any adult to "control" him. That line of thinking can make for a head-on collision between an adult and a child. Montclair lived through that collision over and over again. It would be more than ten years and even more homes before he would settle in with a family that he embraced.

Royletta handled most of the details for Augustine's memorial service. She and I drove to Indianapolis to make arrangements for the funeral. During the ride we discussed our brief second encounter with our mother. My communication with her had been consistent but also distant. We had communicated regularly through mail with cards on each holiday and a letter here or there between. Barbara and I had gone once or twice to visit. Royletta on the other hand had established a closer relationship. They had become friends and she felt a level of grief that was beyond the emotions that I was feeling. My inner being felt a level of guilt and regret. I felt the need to be forgiven, **Exodus 20:12, Honour thy father and thy mother; that thy days may be long upon the land which the Lord thy God giveth thee**. There is no "if", no if they don't mistreat you, no if they don't abandon you, no qualifier for their bad choices or poor decisions, just "Honour thy father and thy mother." No distinction between biological and foster. I told my sister that I felt I hadn't done all that I could have to reach out, and I didn't fully understand why. Royletta told me not to let it get to me or it would consume me. She said that if I really wanted to honor Augustine, I could cover her funeral expense, because no one else was in a financial position to do so. I agreed and I prayed, I prayed for comfort and relief, and true to the Word of the Holy Bible, my prayer was answered. **Isaiah 66:13, As one whom his mother comforteth, so will I**

comfort you; and ye shall be comforted...Psalm 32:1, Blessed is he whose transgression is forgiven, whose sin is covered.

The service was simple and small. Royletta, Michael, Barbara and I were the family members present. Montclair and Robert could not be contacted. I had informed my friends from Indianapolis and they were there, Frank Pace, Mark Artis, Dewayne Richardson and Mark Gibson. A minister and a surprising number of friends of Augustine's that were members of her church were also present. Their being there was both troublesome and relieving. Augustine's friends' presence was troublesome from the stand point that my mother had an entire life with friends and things going on that I was totally unaware of and not a part of. The presence of her friends was relieving from the standpoint that they were evidence that she believed in God and because she believed in God, we would be reunited for a third time. There was something else I felt that was troublesome; Royletta was truly overwhelmed with grief. Within one year's time, the depths of her grief would be revealed.

I asked my sister if she wanted this incident included in my story. She agreed indicating that it may help someone else facing the same situation with the same circumstances. Grief led my sister into a downward spiral that spun her life out of control. One evening in the early fall of the following year, I went to my frat brother's house to watch Monday Night Football. During half time we went to buy more refreshments. On the return home we wanted to avoid traffic lights so we took a side street. As we were approaching a stop sign we noticed a shadow protruding from between the buildings. My frat brother commented that he couldn't believe the "working girls" were out on a night like that one because it was raining and cold. When the car came to a full stop the face of the shadow peered out, it was the shock of my life, that face was Royletta's.

I called her to the car and ordered her into it demanding to know what she was doing, although it was apparent. Then I asked her where she lived. Royletta responded with an address and we started heading there. We rode, without speaking, to the location and finally Royletta broke the silence, "Marsialle, I wasn't standing there because I wanted to be there. I was there because I have a habit and I have to support it. Unless you're going to give me some money, please take me back to where I was. Otherwise, you're just going to make me have to walk in the rain." While I was hurt, I wasn't surprised. My experience with Michael and his use of crack had taught me things, including two new terms, enabler and tough love. I had learned that if I gave her money I was being an enabler, a person that was enabling Royletta to maintain and continue her habit. Tough love would be to do something that is hard to do, but if you really love the person, you do it. I told Royletta that I wouldn't be an enabler; I wouldn't give her money for drugs. I said that I didn't want to see her walk in the rain so I drove her back to the location where she had gotten in the car. As she was about to exit I said, "Royletta I can't give you money for drugs, but I promise you, the day that you want to change, just come to me and I'll be there to help you." She gave me a piercing glare and then said, "I promise you something, I'll never bother you until I want to change," and walked back into the shadows.

I must say that it is truly a tribute to her character, that Royletta kept her word, both parts of it. A countless number of my male friends had allowed their drug habit to rob them of any level of dignity or character. They would knock on the door or call in the middle of the night begging to borrow money. Royletta never communicated with me until she was truly ready to change. Part of the process of tough love is to allow the user to suffer the consequences of their actions until they reach a point that they decide they can't go on in that fashion any longer, and choose to change. The circumstances that led Royletta into a situation that caused her to make the choice were tragic and horrible.

Barbara called me at the office one afternoon and told me that she had received a call from the hospital at Royletta's request. She had been informed that Royletta had been admitted after being brutally beaten, apparently by a John. The attack was so serve that her left eye was damaged beyond repair and would have to be removed. Royletta had called for one reason, she wanted me to get a message; she was ready to change.

After her surgery, Royletta went directly into a rehabilitation facility. After thirty days there, she relocated to South Bend, Indiana to participate in a program operated jointly by the University of Notre Dame and the YWCA. Royletta completed both programs successfully and returned to Gary, Indiana to begin rebuilding her life. First she completed an Associate Degree at Indiana University and then went on to complete the Bachelor of Science degree program. Royletta is a very active member of Narcotics Anonymous and serves as a national officer. Today she is happily married and gainfully employed. I'm so proud of my sister, and her accomplishments. I thank

God that in some small way I was able to be a blessing to my sister. My family and I served as a beacon of hope and an island of stability as she navigated her way through one of the storms of life. I thank God that he heard my prayer. **Psalm 34:4, I sought the Lord, and he heard me, and delivered me from all my fears. Psalm 34:1, I will bless the Lord at all times: his praise shall continually be in my mouth.**

Chapter 21

Our life routine continued to press on, with continued civic involvement and focus on the children. We took on new hobbies like jet-skiing on Lake Michigan. We took a Caribbean Cruise, and did lots of traveling as a family. One of our most enjoyable extracurricular activities was Tee-Ball with the Gary Marlins Youth Sports Team.

Coach Carl Weatherspoon, Coach Ronald Evans, and Coach Jeff Robinson led the team. All three had been my friends and standout athletes during our high school years. Each had gone on to play college sports or Triple-A baseball. In each of their cases, an injury had cut short what could have been, and should have been excellent professional sports careers. After returning home they had each gotten married, and had sons. They started the sports team as an outlet for their own sons. The three of them all enjoyed it so much that they expanded it to become a complete youth sports program that included a tee-ball team, a coach-pitch baseball team, and all the various age brackets for baseball through to high school age. They also had developed a youth basketball program for the various age groups. Spoon, Roll-Aid, and Jeff as we called them were good husbands, good fathers, and good men all around. We enjoyed working with the team so much that I helped to sponsor the uniforms and held several post-game cookouts at our home.

Barbara and I established great relationships with other couples from the Chicago area as well as in Gary, Indiana. Thomas Crump III and his family were very close to ours. We often visited with each other and went out to entertainment events together. They had two beautiful children, a new home and other things in common with us, so we clicked. Thomas and I had gone to the same high school and seemed to have lots of the same ambitions. His father was a very successful man; he was an elected official, a nursing home owner/operator with real estate holdings and other businesses as well. When Mr. Crump senior decided to retire and relocate to Arizona, he dismantled his business empire. One afternoon as Thomas III and I were leaving the golf course he received a call on his new toy, a cellular telephone, the latest technology at the time. It was his father, he needed Thomas III to stop by to sign something, and he told him it was ok if I came along since I was like family. The document that was signed transferred ownership of the two nursing homes to Thomas III and his older sister. With the stroke of a pen, I had witnessed my friend become a millionaire. I was very happy for my friend and I made a promise to myself to work hard so that someday I could have something to pass along to my son.

I continued with my daily and weekly visits to Walter and Uncle George. My relationship with Walter became closer than ever before. Not only was I his "business manager," but also I became his friend and confidant. I knew we were best friends when he asked me to help him select a gift for a friend, a lady friend. It was for her birthday so I suggested a watch. He was relieved to know that I was happy for him and glad that he had moved on with his life.

On one of my visits to Uncle George, I received another shock when I entered the door, this time my brother Montclair sat in the same chair that Aunt Lillian had been setting in. I had not seen Montclair in over 15 years, not since before he had graduated from high school. Montclair stood about 6 foot 3 inches tall, with a weight closer to 300 than to 200 pounds. He stood as I walked toward him and we did a combined shake and embrace. Uncle George said that Montclair had just finished eating some food that he had prepared for him and asked if I was hungry. I said no and that I was on my way home from work and that Barbara would have dinner waiting. "Hey man can I hitch a ride over to Gary with you?" Montclair asked. "Of course," I replied. After a brief chitchat with Uncle George we left.

Once we were on the way our communication opened up. I started things off with the burning question, "Montclair, where have you been?" "Well Marsialle, I've been lots of places, out East, overseas, and most recently, down South." He went on to tell me that after high school, he had also received an academic scholarship to attend Indiana University. After a year of college he left, and entered the military. Once discharged, he, like Michael, had gotten married and had a daughter. His marriage ended in divorce and he moved south. It was there that the new oppressor, crack cocaine, had impacted his life. His addiction eventually led him into a life of crime that resulted in incarceration. He told me the details of the situation and circumstances involved; while incarceration is very serious, the way he described things was quite amusing. It involved him, a lady friend, and an unreturned rented limousine. Let your imagination go wild and you'll get about half of it.

Montclair said he had been released not long ago and used the funds provided when released to travel to Chicago. Montclair said he had been referred to a reentry program that he contacted when he arrived. His description of the program and the conditions were shocking. Those involved were exploited, plain and simple. They were housed in a dormitory and required to wake at 5:30 a.m. each day. After a breakfast of a piece of fruit and a cup of coffee, they were loaded onto vans and taken to various sites along entrance ramps to the freeways. They were given pencils and bags of peanuts to sell to passersby. After twelve hours, they would be picked up, all funds from the day's sales collected, and then returned to the dormitory. Dinner would consist of a hotdog or beef patty, one vegetable and one starch. Lights were turned out at 9:00 p.m. and then do it again the next day. Montclair said he had decided after two weeks, he needed to move on, so he had taken the funds from the day of peanut and pencil sales to cover the cost of a taxi to Uncle George's.

I gave Montclair an update on my situation and circumstances. By the end of the update we were arriving in Gary. I asked Montclair did he have a place to stay and he said that he would be ok if I dropped him off at 11th Ave. and Grant Street. I asked him how was he going to make it and he said that he had learned how to survive on the streets but if I could spot him a few bucks it would help. I said ok and stopped at an Automatic Teller Machine and withdrew $100 and gave it to him. When he saw the amount he said he needed one more favor. I asked what and he told me that one night while passing through Gary, Indiana on his way south he borrowed $40 from his foster mother with a promise that the very next time he was in Gary he would repay her. He wanted to go past her house so he could keep his promise. I agreed and we made the stop.

As I pulled up to the corner of 11th Avenue and Grant Street, I noticed that Lucky's Liquor store was there, and addicts were hanging out in the parking lot. I said to Montclair, "You can't live on the streets forever, what do you plan long-term?" Montclair replied, "One good thing came out of the time in the Pen, I learned a trade. I'm a dental technician. I make false teeth and stuff; I'll get a job in no time when I'm ready for one." With that I gave Montclair my address and telephone number, we embraced and he got out of the car. Montclair was right about his ability to find employment, within three weeks he was working, had an apartment and a live-in lady friend. We stayed in close contact for the next several months, until Montclair stopped by my house to inform me that he would be leaving town on the following day. He said that he would contact me once he settled down in a new location. We sat on the back porch of my house and smoked Cuban cigars that had been given to me by a friend. It was nearly five years before I would have an opportunity to visit with my brother Montclair again.

Chapter 22

The following months would bring change along with an enormous amount of stress attached with it. The first dose of stress came with the passing of Walter's younger sister. Aunt Carrie B. McCormick was the last of his direct descendants and the loss impacted him both emotionally and physically. Walter was now eighty and his health was showing the effects of a battle with inoperable prostate cancer and damaged lungs from years of inhaling the dust created at a cement factory.

The big hit came the Wednesday before Thanksgiving of that year. I stopped in the office to check messages and the fax for an order that I was expecting. There was a communication waiting for me on the fax machine but it wasn't the order that I expected. It was a notification from Dearborn that a decision had been made to close all regional Glass Division offices due to a restructuring of the corporation. The notice indicated that I would be contacted with options in the future. The bottom-line was either relocation or to leave the company.

I spent the next several weeks negotiating with Ford Motor Company Human Resources representatives to determine the fate of my family. Ford offered three different scenarios, a buyout, a demotion to a position at the Chicago Assembly Plant, or relocate to Michigan. The "golden parachute" being offered was very enticing, it included a months' pay for each year I had been with the company, which was thirteen at the time. The funds would be paid on a monthly basis. After the thirteen months of pay, the company guaranteed 50% pay for another 13 months, so long as I proved that I was seeking employment but couldn't find it. I was once told to take the Civil Service employment test once a month and purposefully fail it to collect those funds. Also included would be a year of benefits, i.e. health and life insurance.

There was also the so called, "McDonald's clause" that stated, if after thirteen months I found employment that compensated me at less than 50% of my current pay, the company would supplement that income to bring me to a level of 50% of my current compensation. The idea being that one could take on easy or "light" employment until they reached retirement age. For most of my fifteen coworkers this was a great deal because most were within ten or less years of retirement age with twenty or more years with the company. They would be able to take a job as a ranger at a golf course or something similar and cruise into retirement. I was too young for that, however, the offer seemed like the ideal support program for starting my own business. I spent days investigating the possibility of starting a Manufacturer's Representative Sales business using the contacts that I had established in the glass industry, but concluded that I wanted what I thought would be the security of corporate employment. More than a decade later I would discover there is no true security, the leaders and laws of our government would allow corporations to renege on their promises to employees and customers as well as default on commitments and neglect obligations.

The opportunity to work at the Ford Chicago Assembly Plant seemed like a very viable opportunity. It would allow me to maintain my employment and seniority with the company. I would also be able to avoid relocation, which meant not uprooting the family, and limiting the impact of change to me. Barbara was supportive of this option. She had a great position with the state and was the fourth highest-ranking employee at her location. That meant perks like an assigned parking spot with her name on it. We were considered prominent members of our community and church. Lifelong friends and close family members for camaraderie and support surrounded us. We were on all the social invitation lists, and our son attended the best public elementary school in the city. Life was grand in Gary, Indiana for our family, and Barbara did not want to risk losing everything we had created with the uncertainty and stress of change.

After a visit to the plant and meeting with the leadership, I knew it wouldn't work. In 1995 Ford had several outstanding products on the market including the Taurus, Sable, and Explorer SUV. Each was being built at the Ford Chicago Assembly Plant. The plant operated three shifts and I would be expected to work twelve hours daily as a supervisor, six days per week. The environment was exactly the opposite of what I had experienced over the last thirteen years. The assembly line was dangerous, an injury occurred before my eyes as I was touring the line with the Area Manager. The motorized cart that we were riding was used to carry the injured employee to the infirmary. The Area Manager informed me that I would have a difficult time with both my supervisor and my team. They would know my past as a District Sales Manager, a job that was considered soft and cushy. Therefore I would be "tested" for several weeks, or months, before being accepted as one of the team. My supervisor would have a bit of resentment towards me because my salary would be higher and because I would continue to have a company car while the others in the plant in my position did not get one, including my supervisor. On top of all that, I would need to learn all about manufacturing, of which I had little academic training and basically no experience. To make matters worse, I would lose the management level rank I had worked so hard to earn, and be demoted to the supervisor level, which meant the loss of the company car after three years if I was not promoted within that time frame, which was highly unlikely. I concluded I wouldn't thrive in that environment, which left relocation to Michigan as the only viable option. When I told Barbara of my decision, all hell broke loose.

Our debates over the issue turned into arguments, the arguments turned into shouting matches. Barbara was against a move and particularly to Detroit, which had the distinction of being proclaimed the "Murder Capital of America" by the media. Reports indicated that more murders and crime occurred in Detroit than anyplace else in the country. Also the public school system was rated as one of the worst in the nation; Barbara continually asked why we should move to such a horrible place. My answer was always the same, financial security and to keep what I had worked so hard to gain. I only had good memories of Detroit and my experience there.

I went to Walter to inform him of my decision and to get his opinion. I was pleasantly surprised when he agreed with me. "Marsialle, you're not really a plant kind of guy. You're use to getting there at 8:00 a.m., not 5:00 a.m. You're use to three hour, two martini lunches, not two fifteen minute breaks and a half hour lunch during a 12-hour shift. You don't know anything about a six- day workweek and what that can do to your family life. We sent you off to school to work in an office wearing a suit and necktie, not to work in the plant like me. When you get to Detroit, make sure that your family has everything they have here and more, they'll be just fine. Be the man of the house and take the lead, your family will follow you." I asked Walter would he move there with us so I could continue to be his "business manager" and take care of him. His reply seemed as if he knew that would be the next question and he had an answer prepared. "I'm not ready to move now, maybe in a year or so when I can't take care of myself too much more. So buy a big house that will have enough room for me when I get ready to come." I happily agreed and decided that I would take Dad's advice and take the lead.

I called Ford Motor Company Human Resources the following day to inform them of my decision and finalize arrangements. I was shocked to discover that the "welcome mat" was not out. A meeting was scheduled for later that week, when a representative would fly out to Chicago to meet with me personally to discuss the issue. It was during that week Barbara and I brought things to a head. She stated firmly that she would not move. I responded calmly that she should start looking for a really nice condo for her and Marseille, Jr. to move into because I wouldn't be able to afford both the house and an apartment for myself in Detroit. I told Barbara that I felt in my heart that relocation was best, that I needed to follow my paycheck. I stated that I loved her and didn't want things to end so I had developed a compromise. We would try a commuter marriage. I would work in Detroit and come home every two weeks on the weekend.

As I was sharing my plan with Barbara, we both hadn't noticed that little six-year-old Marseille was listening. He stood and spoke, "Isn't Detroit on that highway I-94, and isn't I-94 right down the street from Grandpa Yearby's house?" he asked. "Yes Emmy," we both replied simultaneously, attempting to reflect a voice of calmness and hoping that our discussion hadn't upset our youngster. "Well it seems to me that we could all go to Detroit and come home anytime we wanted to cause we'll be right down the street from here; it's just a real long street." Barbara and I looked at each other; I smiled and said, "From the mouths of babes." Barbara picked up Marseille Jr. and hugged him. From that point on, our plan became a family relocation to Michigan.

I and Marseille, Jr. – circa 1994

During my meeting with the Ford Human Resources representative I was informed that the intention had never been for me to relocate to Detroit, nor take a demotion into the plant. They had believed that the buyout offer was so good that everyone would take it. They felt with my experience in sales, knowledge of the industry, and contacts in the market, starting my own manufacturer's representative business would be as she put it, "A no-brainer." The disposition of the upper management of Ford Glass Division was that while I was a great salesman and overall good employee, they weren't sure of my ability to thrive and be successful as a business planner in Dearborn. The business planning position was the only opportunity available and the others where graduates from Ivy League colleges with degrees in marketing research, finance, and economics. She told me that my career path had been determined prior to my hire date, and I had been specifically groomed for the position that I was in, and my projected career path no longer existed due to the restructuring.

The conversation that was taking place was difficult for me. The Ford Human Resources representative made things easier by being honest and direct. As I sat there I felt the sensation of the importance of the moment. I wasn't just having a conversation, I was negotiating my future with the company and it wasn't just my future at stake. My family was included, our way of living, our quality of life. I had brought us down this path because I felt it was the right path, the path that God intended so I needed to stay on it. How could I, what could I say or do at that moment that would swing things in not just my, but our favor? It was at that moment that I decided to rely on what I do best. Do what I've always done through the years that have led me to whatever level of success I've achieved, pray for the answer. **Psalm 43:3, O send out thy light and thy truth: let them lead me; let them bring me unto thy holy hill, and to thy tabernacles.**

The Ford Human Resources representative broke our brief silence, "You're a salesman Mr. Arbuckle." There was my answer, she was right, I'm a great salesman, and I needed to sell her a fantastic product; the product was me. As I began my sales pitch I pointed out that I had been a loyal and dedicated employee that had relocated on behalf of the company three times and was now looking to do that a fourth time which would include uprooting my family to do so. I stated that while my advanced degree was not from an Ivy League institution, I did have a Master's of Science degree in Business Management from Central Michigan University, and that the Mid-America

Conference schools are rated as some of the best in the world and Central Michigan was ranked at the top in the conference. I also mentioned that Ford had covered the cost of the degree and that they may want to get a return on their investment.

As with any good sales pitch, the close is the most important element so I went for it. "Those guys that I'll compete against in Dearborn may very well have better credentials than mine. They may even be smarter than me. But I'll tell you one thing they don't have over me, they can't out work me. Even if I have to arrive at 5:00 a.m. each day and leave at 1:00 a.m. each night, I'll get the job done. I stand on a proven track record of success with Ford Motor Company and I deserve a chance. All I want is a chance." The Ford Human Resources representative moved forward in her chair and began arranging the documents on the desk into a blue file folder. She nodded her head a couple of times and then looked me in the eye, "Mr. Arbuckle you're right, you do deserve a chance and I'm going to give you that opportunity. I'll assign you to a business planning position in Dearborn. I'm also going to give you a six month window, if things don't seem like they are going to work out after six months, you can still take the buy-out."

Chapter 23

The remainder of 1994 seemed to zoom by. The holidays were filled with going away dinners and visits. The fact that we were relocating overshadowed everything else that was going on. One highlight of that period was Walter's birthday party that Barbara and I gave for him at our house. Walter's birthday is December 25th, Christmas Day, so it was easy to arrange things. No need for decorating since the house was already decked out with Christmas lights, a Christmas tree and other typical holiday decorations. We put a great deal of effort into assuring that we had invited everyone that we could think of that had a relationship with Walter. We invited his family and extended family, his neighbors, and his friends from his past job and from the church. We also invited some of Barbara's family that had met and made acquaintance with Walter.

The house was packed with people wishing Walter well and enjoying the Yuletide gathering. The event was mostly a dinner party, with lots of food and pleasant conversation. Walter was very pleased and visibly humbled by the fact that so many people thought enough of him to come and participate. I felt proud that I was able to provide the opportunity for Walter to be appreciated and honored. Walter's sister, my Aunt Carrie B. McCormick pulled me to the side and told me how pleased and happy she was that I had chosen to have the event for my father. She said that he had worked hard all his life, mostly to make things good for his family. He deserved a day of recognition and she was pleased that I had provided it. **Deuteronomy 5:16, Honour thy father and thy mother, as the Lord thy God commanded thee; that thy days may be prolonged, and that it may go well with thee, in the land which the Lord thy God giveth thee.**

I, Walter, and the Pastor – Dec. 25, 1994

Within thirty days of the party, Aunt Carrie B. passed away. Because of her age, one cannot say that her death was a shock, but it had a significant impact because she seemed to be in good health and we had just interacted with her at the dinner. Mostly the same family members that were at the party were at her funeral with the addition of a few relatives that had come from out of town. As I scanned the room during her memorial service it was easy to identify the generations of a family that had migrated from the South and reestablished themselves in the Midwest. Nearly every family member there lived in Illinois, Indiana, or Michigan. The roots of the family however were in Georgia where they relocated from during the years of the Great Depression.

Walter was nearly overwhelmed with the loss of his sister. He was now the last survivor of his immediate family. His mother, father, siblings, and wife were all deceased. During the ride from the church to the cemetery he was unusually quiet, making only one comment, "I can't believe it's just me now." I responded, "It's just you, what am I chopped liver?" Walter looked at me, gave a half grin, patted me on the knee and said, "You're a good boy Marsialle."

During that same month I began my transition to the Dearborn, Michigan offices of Ford Glass Division. On Monday morning I would take the three and a half hour drive to Dearborn, Michigan. I would check into the Dearborn Inn hotel, a facility owned by Ford and operated by the Marriot hotel chain. I would then spend the remainder of the day and week at the office 8:00 a.m. to 5:00 p.m., leaving on Friday afternoon to return to Gary, Indiana. In the evenings I would drive around various Detroit suburban areas looking at potential homes and checking out the communities. Barbara had done some research on the Internet and identified Livonia, Michigan as a

143

top choice. Livonia had been recently rated as the third safest city in which to live in America, with the seventh best public school system in the nation. I contacted a real estate agent and began looking at houses.

During the long drives to and from Detroit, I had lots of time to think about and ponder various aspects of life. I spent lots of the time reflecting on the last eight or so years and our life in Gary, Indiana and my career with Ford in Chicago. Things had gone well for the most part and I had been truly successful as a Sales Manager. I thought of what could be called the footnotes of my success, the people that I dealt with. They were truly the reason for my success, but the root cause was my upbringing. I had been raised to be respectful and polite, in particular to those who were my elders. That upbringing served me well during my interface with the various owners, presidents, and general managers that I dealt with. The majority of the businesses were family owned and operated. More often than not the patriarch of the family was the chief decision maker, and usually that person was my father's age and had children my age. While product quality, customer service, and competitive price are key factors in successful selling, if potential customers do not like and respect the salesperson, the salesperson won't be successful. The vast majority of the potential customers liked and respected me because they viewed me as a nice, polite and respectful young man, much like one of their own children.

One example of my being embraced by a company's owner was my relationship with the family that owned Columbia Glass. Albert Hershkoff, his two sisters, his brother-in-law Herman Helfer and, Herman's sons Joel and Harvey, and daughter Gail, all worked for the company. Columbia Glass is a very large and successful glass warehouse and distributorship. Herman was a keen businessman with a jovial personality. He had very low tolerance for those who put on airs or acted like a "big shot." From my first visit I endeared myself to him by being somewhat humble and very respectful. He commented that he couldn't remember the last time a sales representative addressed him with yes and no "sir." I responded that it was how my mom had raised me and he informed me that he and his wife had reared their sons in the same fashion. From that point on, I was an insider. Herman and Albert helped to guide me through the maze of doing business in Chicago and getting paid. Which projects to bid on and which projects were high risk. They also facilitated introductions, even with their competitors and rivals. Can you imagine me playing golf at their country club? Well thanks to Herman and Joel, there I was.

There were many friends that I developed, Jeff at Thermal Dimensions, Ron at Republic, James at Garden City Glass, Steve at Glasstemp and others that extended our relationship beyond the office. We integrated life and work. My family became friends with theirs. We attended weddings, birthdays, funerals and other life events as friends as well as business partners. The years I spent in Chicago were good and productive years and I thank God for the opportunity to have had the experience.

During the last week in January I narrowed the home purchase choices down to three locations with one location as the top choice. The house had everything that our current home had, plus a fourth bedroom, and was twenty years newer construction. Barbara and Marseille Jr. came to Michigan for the weekend to take a look and give approval for the purchase, which they did. An offer was made and accepted, the inspections completed and a closing date set. Everything was falling into place for a successful relocation. I went home the following weekend feeling pleased and in complete control of the situation. That night I went to share the progress and good news with Walter. He was very happy for me and proud that I had figured out a way to maintain my family and my career with Ford. His joy was somewhat subdued by the fact that he had a terrible case of the flu. He said that he had been to the doctor and was taking medicine but that the cold had to run its course and that the worse was over. Yet he was coughing, hacking and spitting between each sentence. I made him some soup, lemon tea, and jello before leaving that evening. The next evening I spent the entire evening with Walter. We watched the NBA All-Star game and I did a bit of cleaning around the house. At one point his coughing got so bad that I suggested he go to the hospital. He declined and once again pointed out that a cold or the flu has to run its course and that the worst was over.

The following morning I left for Michigan, I thought of checking on Walter on the way out of town, but I was running a bit behind schedule so I immediately hit the highway. I asked Barbara to check on him on her way to and from work each day. I arrived at the Dearborn Inn and checked in as usual. When I got to my room the message light on the telephone was flashing. I thought to myself, "Who could be calling me?" since very few people know I'm here. The folks at the office must need something I thought, so I picked up the phone. The front desk indicated that I had just received a call from home; it must have been while I was on the elevator, and to call immediately. When I called, Barbara answered the phone in a trembling and tearful voice. "Marsialle I went over to Mr. Yearby's house like you asked me, and I found him on the front porch on his knees like he was praying, but he was dead!" "I'll be home as soon as I can get there," were the only words that I could utter. I picked up my travel bag off the bed, went down to the front desk and asked to check out. As the clerk prepared the invoice for my signature my eyes began to fill with tears; as I signed the receipt a tear fell onto the document and the clerk asked if everything was ok. I wiped my eyes, nodded my head and said "Yes, but I'm never going to stay here again." To this day I have never again set foot inside the Dearborn Inn.

The drive home was long and difficult. I thought of my entire life and the time spent with Walter. I thought of times we spent fishing and hunting. Hanging out together, going to watch baseball games and high school football games. The few times that he had yelled at me and the one time he had spanked me. I thought of the advice that he had given me on everything from love and marriage to child rearing and finances. I thought of the fact that all of his advice was backed with the proven example he had of life experience, with a proven track record of success. Walter had been more than just a father; he was a friend and confidant. He was my "ace in the hole" and my "backup plan," now I felt like it was just me.

Proverbs 4:1-2, Hear, ye children, the instruction of a father, and attend to know understanding. For I give you good doctrine, forsake ye not my law. My reflections then shifted, I began to ponder the bits and pieces of advice and training that had developed me into the man that I had become. During my childhood certain character traits were drilled into me by various means, one of which was Scouting. Walter had made sure that both my brother Michael and I were in the Cub Scouts and Boy Scouts of America programs in our community. The scouting programs were run by Mr. Glover, a community activist, and Mr. Washington, who was a neighbor two doors down from our home. Mrs. Warren and Mrs. Williams were the Den Mothers for the Cub Scouts. They all had children in our age group that were friends and classmates at school. Each week we met in the gymnasium of Banneker Elementary School. Before the weekly activity began we would all line up in military rank and file to recite the Scout Oath, and more importantly, because of how they were drilled into our memories, the Scout Motto, and Scout Law:

The Motto: **"Be prepared!"**

The Law: **"A Scout is trust-worthy, loyal, helpful, friendly, courteous, kind, obedient, cheerful, thrifty, brave, clean, and reverent."**

The motto is a simple two-word phrase and the law simply consists of twelve adjectives. Yet they are two words and twelve adjectives that could define an individual and the quality of life that they and the others that they encounter experience. At the time that I was committing them to memory I didn't understand the significance or long-term impact that they would have on my life. As I drove along I-94 I promised myself that I would always be prepared to take advantage of any positive opportunity that comes my way. I also committed myself to exemplify the twelve laws in my day to day living.

Proverbs 4:14-15, Enter not into the path of the wicked, and go not in the way of evil men. Avoid it, pass not by it, turn from it, and pass away. Walter also believed in standing on the side of what was right, which is not always easy to do. He firmly believed that if you stand on the principle of what is morally and ethically right, then ultimately you will win, because what is right always tops what is wrong, or as Walter put it, "Wrong can be strong but right is the might that can overcome the strong of the wrong." To illustrate his belief he often told us his version of the stories of Camelot. He made King Arthur the hero and Sir Lancelot the villain because of his betrayal of Arthur for the love of Guinevere. Walter reinforced the notion that being trust-worthy and loyal are key ingredients to good relationships.

The more I reflected on Walters's life, the more I found myself hoping that I could do as well in life as he had. Despite my life's beginning, I had all the advantages when compared to Walter. I had the opportunity to obtain a great education from a top academic institution, Walter had none. Yet, he had fully lived the American dream. He had served his country, worked for over thirty years until retirement, purchased a home and paid for it. Walter, a man that could not read nor write had financed major home improvements, automobiles and maintained an excellent credit rating. He had raised two children and sent them both off to college. In his death he left Michael and me an inheritance, and we were living legacies and evidence of his existence. Would I accomplish as much as

Walter became a repeating question, along with the question of how?

The answer was and still is hard work, and I smiled as I thought of how Walter and Rosie had stated it as plainly as that over the years. Their approach for success was a reflection of their religious, cultural and socio-economic middle-class peer group, which were the members of the Christian Methodist Episcopal Church. The CME's held their first General Conference in 1870; the members are the only major denomination established in the outset as an independent body by former slaves. Originally the word "Colored" stood in place of the word "Christian". They are proud men and women, proud of who they are and where they come from. They believe that one's potential is not necessarily predicted by one's past.

One of those former slaves was Isaac Lane, who became a Bishop of the CME Church. Bishop Lane stated that he knew that there was a world in which African-Americans were denied the opportunity to learn broadly without any role models to inspire the rising generations. With that vision in mind Lane established the then CME High School, which later became Lane College. Today Lane College is a top HBCU and is a crown jewel of the C.M.E. Church.

Lane College men and women are taught to be confident and assertive. The men in particular are taught to be refined, tender toward the bashful, gentle towards those who would be strangers and understanding of their differences. He is trained to easily connect to those with whom he is speaking. He learns to shun slander and gossip. He is taught never to be mean spirited and not to take advantage of others. He is instructed to remember the teaching of his elders. He is trained to be patient and capable of enduring much pain. He learns that his sympathies are to be infinite, he is taught that his charity should know no end, and that arrogance is an ugly trait. Those aspects of character and ideology were passed to me from Walter and Rosie at home as well as by most of the folks that were a part of my social circle, other CME's. **Proverbs 22:1-2, A good name is rather to be chosen than great riches, and loving favour rather than silver and gold. The rich and poor meet together: the Lord is maker of them all.**

After what seemed like a full lifetime my drive ended. Barbara met me with tears and hugs. I knew that finding my father was a traumatic experience for her so I waited until the next day to have any discussion of the details. Barbara did want to talk about the position that she found him in, on his knees, out on the closed-in front porch. I told her that he had probably gone out to pray and had a heart attack and could not get up. Later we would learn that it had been a stroke that occurred. The rest of the night we just held each other and cried.

The next day we began the process of making the arrangements. There was so much that had to be done: telephone the mortuary, go to the coroner's office, phone calls to family and friends, visit a lawyer about the will, make arrangements for the memorial service, call a barber, select a suit, select a shirt, select a necktie, select a casket, write the obituary, take it to the printer, call the florist, call and meet with the minister, call the musician, pack up the house, contact Walter's car insurance and other business accounts, close credit card accounts, contact the pension fund and social security offices. The process consumed all of our time and thoughts

The funeral service had an eerie level of familiarity to it. We had all just come together a month or so earlier for Aunt Carrie B.'s funeral and now here we were funeralizing her brother Walter. All the same faces just a different location. After the funeral we had a reading of the will, which revealed that Walter and Rosie had made the decision to leave all of their worldly possessions to Michael and me, half to each, many years ago. Michael and I decided we would keep the house and rent it out for a few years. I took Dad's television, one of his most prized possessions, a floor model color 32" Zenith. It still sits in my basement and still operates after a 15 minute or so warm up period. **Proverbs 3:1-2, My son, forget not my law; but let thine heart keep my commandments: For length of days, and long life, and peace, shall they add to thee.**

Chapter 24

We completed our transition to Michigan by mid-April. Thus began a whirlwind of change and positive growth. Within a year I changed Divisions within Ford from Glass Division to Climate Control Division. I progressed from Business Planner to Product Manager leading the radiator team. Barbara landed a new position with a major non-profit which doubled her salary from the position she held in Gary, Indiana. Marseille, Jr. was accepted into the advanced student placement program for academically gifted children within our local school system.

A couple of years more and things progressed more. I received a promotion to join the team that would launch Ford's new spinoff Visteon. This represented a major salary increase. Barbara changed jobs and joined another non-profit in a key leadership position, which represented an income boost. Marseille, Jr. was doing great academically in middle school; he was also in the starting rotation as a pitcher on the city All Star Little League Baseball travel team.

In 1998 we were blessed with an opportunity to travel to Europe. Barbara's sister was serving in the military and stationed in Kaiserslautern, Germany. We made her home our base as we traveled throughout the region over a two and a half week period. During that time we visited Frankfurt and explored the German countryside. We also went to Paris, France, Holland and Amsterdam along with other cities in the Netherlands. I visited with some of my Omega Psi Phi fraternity brothers that are stationed there and active with our International Chapter. The brothers arranged for me to have the privilege of playing golf on the course at Ramstein Air Base. In order to get there I had to drive a car and experience the infamous European Autobahn. While I played golf that day, Barbara and her sister Andrea went to Belgium and purchased crystal ware. We also attended the North Sea Jazz Festival in The Hague while Marseille, Jr. went to Euro Disney which is just outside of Paris with our niece and nephew, Shenae and Andre.

After we returned home I discovered that there was one person from our family that needed to become a part of our life in Michigan, Uncle George. My weekly visits had transitioned to twice weekly phone calls. Living alone in the large house that he and Aunt Lillian built had become too much for him to manage so he decided to move to a senior citizens high rise apartment on the South Side of Chicago near his home. After a year or so he determined that he didn't like it. We therefore agreed that he would move to Michigan and live with us.

After a short period Uncle George decided he didn't like life at our house because it was too lonely during the day. Barbara, Marseille, Jr. and I all left home for school and work by 7:30

a.m. No one returned until after 4:00 p.m., therefore he was alone all day. We suggested adult daycare, but George felt a retirement village would be better. He would be around people his own age and could make friends. They would have planned activities for him and the others to participate in, along with on-sight healthcare. Uncle George said he also wanted to be practical; he could progress to assisted-living or fulltime care when required. There was a facility just across town from us, only a ten minute drive. Uncle George decided he would live there and we could visit him daily. We all agreed and put the plan into action. Things worked out well, between Barbara and me, we visited Uncle George each day. He often went to church with us as well as to Marseille, Jr.'s little league games and had dinner at our house on Sundays and holidays.

It was through my daily visits to Uncle George that I developed a relationship with members of Livonia American Legion Post 32. It was located directly across the street from Uncle George's place. One day while visiting Uncle George, I was informed that Uncle George began to stumble while attempting to walk regularly, even with a cane or walker and we should consider getting Uncle George a wheelchair. As I was leaving I noticed members of the American Legion Post Honor Guard practicing drills in the parking lot, and thought to myself I remembered reading somewhere that they have a wheelchair program for veterans. I decided to stop and ask.

I approached a gentleman that was shouting out the commands, excused myself for interrupting and asked him about enrolling Uncle George in the wheelchair program. He asked if I had anything that could verify my Uncle's status as a veteran and I said yes. I happened to have Uncle George's veteran administration identification card in my wallet from another time I filled out documents for Uncle George and had not returned it. I handed it to the man and he said I'll be right back as he walked toward the entrance to the facility which is a brown brick single story building that resembles a restaurant or nightclub from the exterior. Half of the building is a banquet facility and the other half is a bar where veterans and seniors gather daily.

I assumed he was going to get the application or other paper work for me to complete, instead he returned with a brand new wheelchair with the tags still hanging on it and pushed it to me as he handed me Uncle George's Veteran Administration identification card. "How much will this cost," I ask. "Nothing, the only thing that we ask is that you return the wheelchair to us when your uncle no longer can use it or needs it. We can have it refurbished and provide it for someone else." I was shocked and humbled. The following day I returned and asked was there anything that I could do to help the organization, maybe a donation or something. I was informed that by virtue of my being a direct descendant of a veteran I was eligible to become a member of the Sons of the American Legion. I joined and have participated and maintained my membership for the last twelve years. I have served as Chaplain and Manager of the youth baseball program for the Sons of the American Legion of Livonia American Legion Post 32. I also have the distinction of being Post 32's only African American member, in its history of existence.

Uncle George's health declined steadily and the last holiday meal that he enjoyed with us, and us with him, was Thanksgiving 1999. He was blessed to live into the new millennium but passed away in February of 2000. We returned him to Chicago for his memorial service and burial alongside Aunt Lillian. The members of his church, Saint James African Methodist Episcopal Church, were very gracious and kind to us. Rev. J. L. Thorn and the congregation extended themselves and the facility to our family and we were very appreciative. It also reflected well on the legacy of George's life and the relationship that he had with his friends and peers. Although George had not lived in Chicago for nearly four years, the church was filled to capacity for his funeral. When I reflect on the entire episode of caring for Uncle George, I know that Uncle George himself made it pleasant and easy. He was soft spoken and agreeable. He was realistic and unattached to material possessions. He was considerate of the impact that caring for him had on us and seemed to be more sensitive to our needs as caregivers than to his own needs.

Chapter 25

Within a couple of more years I was elected to the position of Chairman of the Board of Directors of our church's multimillion dollar federally funded Head Start program and also appointed to the Board of Directors for another multimillion dollar non-profit, Michigan Neighborhood Partnership, a fiduciary that distributes federal grant money to faith based and community groups for their programs. At work I had become the editor to FAAN Mail, a corporate newsletter that expressed the issues and concerns of the Ford African Ancestry Network. Along with that responsibility there was the task of attending a wide variety of banquets and formal dinners as a representative of the Ford Motor Company. At those events Barbara and I met and made the acquaintance of many celebrity and notable people. Marseille, Jr. was performing excellently academically in school, he was playing the coronet in the school band as I had done, and he was well on his way to becoming an Eagle Scout. As a result I took on the role of working with the Boy Scouts of America corporate fundraising team.

The blessings continued to flow more and more. I was able to facilitate a gift of $18,000 from Ford Motor Company to our church's Scouting program. That was the largest corporate gift ever presented to our church. The funds were utilized to cover the cost of sending Marseille, Jr. and our entire Boy Scout Troop to the International Scouting Jamboree, making them the first all African American Boy Scout Troop to attend the International Jamboree in the history of Scouting. As a result of our salaries and controlled spending, (I must give Barbara the majority of the credit for that) we were able to afford a small yacht, and touring motorcycle, and a 1974 Fiat Spider convertible antique sports car. For our anniversaries Barbara and I traveled to Hawaii, New York, San Diego, Miami, Toronto, and Las Vegas. She and I also took cruises to Jamaica, the Bahamas, Tortola, and the British West Indies. We also took Marseille, Jr., Jamillah, and Rodney on a family cruise aboard Warner Brothers' Big Red Boat to St. Thomas, St. Martin, and St. Croix along with a visit to Disney World in Orlando, FL. Marseille, Jr. and I took the yacht across Lake Erie to several ports along the Ohio coast including Cedar Point Amusement Park for a never to be forgotten father and son sea adventure.

Barbara & I in our vintage 1974 Fiat Spider – summer 2000

Life was grand! My career was being enhanced with lots of travel to Mexico, Brazil, Venezuela, and Canada. I, along with some co-workers and friends, also launched the International Networking Consortium. The consortium sponsored an event each third Friday of the month bringing together individuals from across the automotive industry for sharing best practices and career enhancement advice. I was also active and holding an office on the district level (multi-state responsibility) in the administration of both my fraternity, Omega Psi Phi, and my lodge, the Grand United Order of Odd Fellows. With lots of responsibility there is lots of work, and the consumption of lots of time and energy. There were meetings daily after work, and days that began at 4:30 a.m. and ended at midnight or later.

The weekends did not mean rest; they meant travel, setups and breakdowns, and hardcore partying, with lots to eat and lots to drink.

It all came to a head on Wednesday, June 26, 2003. That was the date of the International Freedom Festival Fireworks on the Detroit River, sponsored by Detroit, MI and Windsor, Ontario. The marina hosted a major party that night in conjunction with the event. There was a band, barbeque, and lots of people. We had the entire family at the marina for the occasion. My daughter Jamillah and her husband Theo, our grandchildren, Rodney and Noah, (Jonah had not been born yet) my son Marseille, Jr. and my wife Barbara were all there. The next day was to be my last day at the office for two weeks, after which would be a much needed vacation. I had noticed that I was feeling extra tired and fatigued over the last few days, but attributed it to high stress and the long hours I was keeping.

I had made the decision not to drink much alcohol that night because of an early meeting scheduled at the office the next day. I also decided that I would spend the night at the marina and packed an overnight bag with the outfit that I would wear to work the next day. The rest of the family was scheduled to go home that night. As the evening progressed, I played with the kids, ate several Italian and Polish sausages, and watched the fireworks with the family all gathered around. As the night drew to a close, the family packed up and headed home while I headed off to the boat to lie down at around 11:00 p.m. The party at the marina was in full swing and things were loud and raucous. After about twenty minutes of attempting to sleep I made a decision that resulted in being a life saving change of mind. I decided to go home, feeling that I would get a better night of rest there, even if I had to get up a little earlier to get to the office the next day.

My drive home was normal and I found things as usual when I arrived home. Within thirty minutes I was comfortably tucked into bed and resting peacefully. The next morning when I woke at 6:00 a.m. and I swung my feet over the edge of the bed, as they touched the floor, I suffered a massive heart attack. The pain was piercing and snatched my breath away. It felt as if a four hundred pound weight had been dropped on my chest. It forced me to crouch over and grab at my chest.

At first I thought that I had an urgent need to use the toilet. Within moments I knew that wasn't the case. I said to Barbara, "Honey, I'm having chest pain!" "I'll call 911," she said with a voice of exasperation. I could only say "Ok." I thought to myself, "Let me get down stairs so the paramedics won't have to drag my big butt down the steps." I stumbled down the stairway clutching my chest, and counting each of the thirteen steps trying to use that as a diversion. By the time I reached the foyer at the bottom of the stairway a second wave of major pain struck. It felt as if a second weight had been dropped on my chest. The impact of the pain was so intense that it made me weak in the knees and I felt a rush of nausea come over me. I staggered to the restroom in the hallway and regurgitated in the toilet.

I again staggered to the foyer to await the arrival of the paramedics. I realized that I was standing there in only a pair of gym shorts that I had slept in. I looked up and saw Marseille, Jr. standing at the top of the stairway with a horrified look on his face. I ask him to throw me down a tee shirt, which he did. As I pulled the shirt over my head I attempted a deep breath, but another wave of pain hit. The intensity was so powerful that I bent over and grabbed at my chest. I concluded that breathing increased the pain so I attempted to hold my breath for bit. I staggered to the front door and opened it so that I could see the ambulance when it arrived. It was time to take another breath. The pain hit with the breath and tears filled my eyes. I thought to myself, maybe if I sit down so I staggered over to the sofa and sat down, no relief. I laid back, no relief. I stood again, and it was time to take another breath, and more pain. I decided that I could not withstand the pain of another breath, so I would hold it until I passed out. At that moment the ambulance drove up.

I burst through the door and stumbled out onto the lawn. I yelled to the paramedic as he stepped from the vehicle, "It's me, I'm the victim, and I'm having a heart attack!" He grabbed me by my arm and assisted me over to and into the ambulance. There was a second paramedic inside. They helped me lay on the cot and began speaking to me in a noticeably calm and a matter of fact voice. "What symptoms are you experiencing?" he asked as he was connecting EKG wires to me. "My chest feels like ten men are standing on it!" The second paramedic was calling into the hospital and informing them of my vital signs. "The EKG indicates that you do appear to be experiencing cardiac arrest. The first thing that we are going to do is attempt to reduce the pain and stabilize you so that we can transport you to a hospital." I nodded my head to indicate that I understood. "I'm going to place a small tablet of nitroglycerin under your tongue. If your pain is at a level ten now, describe the level you're at as the tablet dissolves." "No change," I said. After four tablets I felt relief to a level 6 and we were on our way to St. Mary's Hospital around the corner from the house.

We arrived in approximately four minutes. As soon as I was wheeled into the cardiac emergency unit, the nurse cut away the shirt that I had put on earlier. That act seemed to set the stage and define the meaninglessness of possessions and everything else in the world at that moment. Only my survival was critical and important. To live was the only thing that mattered. I knew that this situation had become a life or death moment. A new wave of pain hit and I groaned and grimaced.

The nurse asked me to stretch my arms out so that an IV could be started in both arms, she also said, in a loud voice, "Mr. Arbuckle have you taken or used any non-prescription or illegal drugs?" "No," I responded with a grunt. "Do you take any prescription medication?" "Yes, Atenolol for high blood pressure, aghh." "Mr. Arbuckle we're going to see if we can get control of the pain, first I need to give you a digital rectal exam, please roll over onto your side." "I'm having a heart attack; my heart is in my chest, what are you checking back there for?" "We may be giving you some blood thinners and we have to make sure you don't have any rectal bleeding." I frowned and groaned as I turned to my side. After the nurse completed her exam, another nurse entered the room with two large syringes and four small valves of medicine on a silver tray. "Mr. Arbuckle, I'm going to administer some medication to see if we can control and eliminate some of the pain. I have morphine here and I believe that will do the job." Bamm, as the nurse injected the morphine I could feel an immediate sensation of relief and euphoria. It seemed as if calmness crept over my entire body and the room as well. Whoosh! "How does that feel?" the nurse asks. "Wonderful, may I have some more please," I said with a smile, but I was sincere with my request. "In just a moment, how is your pain level?" "About a two, or maybe a one and a half," I said as I realized that I did actually feel much better. "Ok, we're going to inject some on the other side and then we'll be doing an ultrasound on your heart so we can take a look at things." Bamm; whoosh!

A young male nurse entered the room wheeling in a large device that he used to do the ultrasound. I remember him pressing extremely hard on my chest and saying that because of my body mass he wasn't sure that his reading was accurate. After a second attempt a look of extreme concern came over him. He scurried out of the room and reentered with a doctor and they both looked at the screen. "What is it?" I asked. "You appear to have a serious blockage in the left ventricle. The extreme pain that you're experiencing is due to the lack of blood getting to that portion of the heart. The time has now become an issue, time represents heart damage. You need cardiac catheterization; the issue is that we're not certified to perform that procedure here so we need to transport you to another facility. We'll go to work on that right now." It was time for more morphine, bamm; whoosh!

As I lay there alone I began to pray:

> God, I don't want to die. I'm really not ready to die yet. But, if it is my time to go, thank you for the wonderful life that you allowed me to live. I can't be mad, because you've let me have a great run at it.

But I don't want to die; I'm not ready to die.

If it is my time, please take care of Barbara, Marseille, Jr., Jamillah and her family, my sister and brothers and nieces and nephews and everybody. Bless them and watch over them.

God, I don't want to die and I'm really not ready to die.

But if it is my time, please forgive me for all of my sins and take me into heaven.

But God, I don't want to die and I'm not ready to die.

In the name of your son Jesus Christ I pray. Amen

Barbara and Marseille, Jr. entered the room and stood against the wall in the corner. Within moments Jamillah and Theo entered the room also. They were standing there looking and wondering just as I, how is this going to turn out? The nurse entered the room and began speaking to and looking at Barbara but her voice volume allowed me to hear the conversation. "Because of the rain and high winds and low cloud cover, we can't seem to find a helicopter service that will transport Mr. Arbuckle to another facility that has cardiac catheterization certification." "What? What do you mean?" Barbara asked in a horrified tone. "They won't fly. We can't find one that will risk the flight." "We have insurance that will cover this, call an ambulance. I have a brand new car, I'll drive him myself in my own damn car!" Barbara shouted. "Madame, Mrs. Arbuckle," the nurse said looking Barbara directly in the eyes and placing her hands on either side of Barbara's arms, "We've got sixteen to twenty minutes left for transport, an ambulance, your car, no vehicle would make it in time, and besides the trauma would be too great. The helicopters just won't fly. We've done all we can do and now we're going to make Mr. Arbuckle as comfortable as we possibly can." With that the nurse walked out of the room and Barbara began to walk towards me.

As Barbara looked down over me, her eyes filled with tears. She began to lean forward to give me what I knew was to be the "Good-Bye" kiss. As she got close enough for me to feel her breath against my skin something stirred inside me and I slid my hand between my face and hers and said, "Don't kiss me good-bye, I'm not done fightin' yet," as I gently pushed her away. "I'm not done fightin' and I need to draw on your strength, so go to the restroom and wash your face and pull yourself together. Go ahead now, go on." Barbara rose up batting the tears away in her eyes with a half grin, "Ok baby, I'll be right back." "Jamillah, Theo, go give her a hand. Emmy, (my nickname for Marseille, Jr.) come over here." He walked over and looked at me with almost a blank stare. "Dad might not make it through this one. If I don't, I want you to remember this number, 60-75-31. That's the combination to the safe. You'll find a bunch of papers, go through them and you will find some savings bonds, stock certificates, titles to the cars, motorcycle, boat, and jet-ski. There will also be some cash and the insurance policies. Your name is listed as the beneficiary on a lot of that stuff; Mom's name is on the rest. Don't sign anything for six months or so, that'll give everyone and everything time to settle down. Stick with Mom and keep the family together, Ok?" "Ok Dad."

As Barbara, Jamillah, and Theo reentered the room, the nurse entered behind them. Once again she had the two large syringes. "Time to feel good Mr. Arbuckle," she said in a light and cheery voice as if all was well. She steps on my left side and administered the injection, bamm; whoosh. The nurse then began walking over to my right side, looking at my right outstretched hand the nurse made notice of my college graduation class ring and in a light tone one would use to stimulate a response she said, "Umm, Indiana University, huh?" It was then that the Lord moved in His mysterious way, His wondrous miracles to perform. He motivated me to make my response a reflection of my pride and self-confidence; along with the pride of generations of hard working African Americans. I responded, "Yeah, that's a Big Ten school."

With my completion of the sentence you could see the light bulb go off in the mind of the nurse. She dropped the syringe and immediately ran from the room to the telephone on the counter just outside the door. I could hear click, click, click, ten times as the telephone buttons made the tapping sound from her quickly pressing each one. "Hello, U of M Hospital, we have a Big Ten Alumni here, will you send over the Survival Unit?" They arrived within seven minutes!

The University of Michigan Survival Flight team looked like super heroes as they entered the room. They wore bright blue jumpsuits and gold colored helmets with gold reflective visors that covered their entire face. It seemed as if they removed and switched the IV's from the hospital equipment to theirs and put me in the helicopter in one motion. The space was small, there was only the pilot, co-pilot, and me with a nurse seated at my side and a nurse seated at my head. "Have you ever flown in a helicopter before Mr. Arbuckle," a nurse asked. "No," I replied. "Well we want you to enjoy this flight, so we're going to inject you with some morphine." Bamm; whoosh! I remember looking out of the window and seeing the treetops and thinking to myself that I didn't recognize the area below. "How is your flight so far Mr. Arbuckle?" "Fine," I replied. "Well, we want to be sure that this is your best ever, so we're going to give you some more morphine," the nurse said back to me. Bamm; whoosh!

My next memory is seeing the group of doctors on the hospital helipad waiting for us from the window. It seemed as if they began prepping me for surgery as we rolled down the corridor to the operating room, "Mr. Arbuckle we're going to do a catheterization and explore the left side of your heart. If possible we'll do angioplasty, if not you'll require open heart." Next I could feel the pressure on my groin as the catheter was inserted. "Mr. Arbuckle if you'll look up to your left, you can see inside your artery on the monitor," a voice said from behind the gauze mask in front of me. The only portion of the face visible was the eyes and brow of the speaker. The eyes looked sincere and knowledgeable. "What's your name?" "I'd like to know your name since you're operating on me," I asked. "Garg, I'm Dr. Garg, and I'm going to press the probe against this blockage here to see if it penetrates, and it does." Mr. Arbuckle we're going to clear your blockage and place a stent inside your left ventricle afterwards, in fact I believe you'll require two stents because of the length of the distance that we have to clear. We don't want your artery to collapse. You can go to sleep now. You're going to be ok."

When I woke I was in a hospital room with my wife sitting by my side. She was sitting there with her eyes closed maybe praying, maybe nodding. I felt great! No pain, no shortness of breath. "Barb," I said with a sense of happiness that I had survived. "Marsialle, how do you feel," Barbara asked as she moved toward me and then leaned forward and gave me a warm embrace. "You scared us!" "I scared me too, baby," I said as I hugged her back. **Psalm 116:1-8, I LOVE the Lord, because he hath heard my voice and my supplications. Because he hath inclined his ear unto me, therefore I will call upon him as long as I live. The sorrows of death compassed me, and the pains of hell gat hold upon me: I found trouble and sorrow. Then I called upon the name of the Lord; O Lord I beseech thee, deliver my soul. Gracious is the Lord, and righteous; yea, our God is merciful. The Lord preserveth the simple: I was brought low, and he helped me. Return unto rest, O my soul; for the Lord has dealt bountifully with thee. For thou hast delivered my soul from death, mine eyes from tears, and my feet from falling.**

Chapter 26

Over the next three or four months I recuperated at home. Most of the time was spent learning all about heart disease, its cause, and impacts. Cardiac rehabilitation and working with a cardio-physiologist to reduce my cardiovascular risk factors was also a major part of my activity. I was surprised to discover that although I was on the go all of the time, my lack of exercise and overweight condition was a major contributor to my heart failure. I learned how exercise could keep my heart healthy. Increasing my physical activity would:

- Reduce the risk of additional heart disease
- Improve blood flow through my body
- Help lower the risk of a stroke
- Help lower my cholesterol
- Help to keep my blood pressure down
- Help reduce my risk of developing diabetes
- Help me to lose weight, which would reduce the amount of hard work my heart has to do

- Help control blood sugar levels

The decision to start exercising was easy, but getting started wasn't. I followed the tips provided by the American Heart Society for starting an exercise program:

- **Check with you healthcare provider**. – Before you begin any type of exercise plan, always talk to your healthcare provider first. He or she can tell you which exercise is safe for you. Especially if you have heart disease, or diabetes, or if you are overweight.
- **Easy does it**. - If you've never been active, keep it short. Start with only 5 to 10 minutes of exercise. Then, slowly build up to longer sessions – 30 minutes a day 3 to 4 times a week.
- **Be comfortable**. – Wear properly fitting sneakers and loose clothing that suits the weather.
- **Warm up**. – Start and finish with a low-level activity or stretching. It will make exercise safer and more comfortable.
- **Make exercise a habit**. – Exercise at the same time each day. And, before you know it, exercise will become a part of your lifestyle.
- **Build it into your daily life**. – Make exercise a part of your everyday life. For example, walk to buy your newspaper every morning.
- **Exercise with a friend or family member**. – Try going for a bike ride with your best friend. It may be far more motivating than going alone.

- **Choose fun activities**. – The more you enjoy them, the more likely you are to stick with them.
- **Join an exercise group**. – Check with your local YMCA, community centers, and places of worship.
- **Drink water**. – Before, during, and after exercise. However, check with your healthcare provider first. Some people need to monitor their fluid intake.
- **Keep track**. – Write down what you did and how long you spent doing it.
- **Last but not least, Don't Over Do It**! – Do low to moderate exercises. Remember, start slowly. Then, build up gradually.

I decided that walking would be my exercise of choice. It was easy, and I didn't need to learn anything new. I wouldn't need any special equipment besides a comfortable pair of shoes. Best of all, I could do it anytime, anywhere. I started by just going to the corner and back, then around the block, then the subdivision, and finally 3 to 5 miles daily. I was amazed with the fact that I lost over 45 pounds along the pathways that I walked.

Walking also provided lots of time for thought. I focused mostly on the major events that had occurred during my lifetime and the tremendous impact African Americans had made during my 45 years of existence. Extraordinary men and women had invented things, blazed trails, transformed misconceptions, and rewritten record books. One of the many books that I read during that period of time was *Profiles of Great African Americans*. I had received an autographed copy of the book by one of the co-authors, Stan West, which I had the pleasure of meeting at the National Black MBA Association Conference a couple of years earlier. I would think of the individuals that I had read of the evening prior to my walk. I thought of;

- **Hank Aaron** – Despite racial abuse, derogatory threat letters, and death threats, Hank hit his 715th home run on April 8, 1974 to break Babe Ruth's record.
- **Dr. Charles G. Adams** – Dr. Adams attended Fisk University and graduated with honors from The University of Michigan and Harvard Divinity School. After serving as Pastor of Concord Baptist Church in Boston, New England's largest African American Church he began leadership of Detroit's Hartford Memorial Baptist Church. His dynamic leadership and vision has led to the development of numerous charitable and community outreach ministries including a Head Start Program, Hunger Task Force, Daily Senior Citizens Program, REACH Program for AIDS awareness and Child Visitation Program for incarcerated mothers, just to name a few. He is noted as one of America's 100 Most Influential African Americans.
- **Muhammad Ali** – Considered by most as the greatest heavyweight boxer of all time, Ali won 56 fights with only 5 defeats before he retired as the first boxer to win the Heavyweight Championship 3 times.

- **Marian Anderson** – The first African American singer to solo with New York's Metropolitan Opera. Perhaps her greatest concert came before my birth, when she sang Easter morning on the steps of the Lincoln Memorial after being denied the opportunity to sing at Constitution Hall in Philadelphia by the Daughters of the American Revolution in 1935.

- **Louis Armstrong** – Internationally known for his trumpet playing and jazz singing, his technical mastery and improvisational innovation changed the course of jazz music and influenced the style of many other musicians.

- **James Baldwin** – One of the most widely read and popular African American writers, he used his sensitivity to honestly examine race, gender, and class distinctions. His major works include the novel *Go Tell It on the Mountain* and the essay collections *Notes of a Native Son* and *The Fire Next Time.*

- **Gwendolyn Brooks** – The first African American to win a Pulitzer Prize of any kind for her book of poetry titled *Annie Allen.* Later she was appointed Poet Laureate for the State of Illinois, poetry consultant to the Library of Congress and received a Lifetime Achievement Award from the National Endowment for the Arts.

- **James Brown** – A two time Grammy Award winner, he was one of the most popular and influential performers in the history of America. He was also an astute businessman. His songs reflected growing racial pride, his hit "Say It Loud I'm Black and I'm Proud," became a new Black national anthem.

- **Ralph Bunche** – The first African American to hold a Ph.D. in political science from Harvard University and the first African American to hold a key post with the State Department as a specialist on African Affairs. He mediated a major conflict resolution in the Arab-Israeli War of 1948 and rose to the post of Under Secretary of the United Nations. Bunche also received a Nobel Peace Prize. In addition he established the Political Science Department at Howard University.
- **Shirley Chisholm** – The first African American Congresswoman. She was also the first woman to make a serious bid for the White House.
- **Bill Cosby** – An award winning comedian that has recorded more than 30 albums and was the first African American to star in a network television drama series.
- **Thomas Dorsey** – The most prolific composer of Gospel Music. He wrote and published more than 1,000 songs including the renowned "Precious Lord, Take My Hand."
- **W. E. B. Du Bois** – Thought of as one of the greatest Black intellectuals of this century, he helped to found the NAACP. He was a pioneer in sociology, history, and anthropology, along with being a major contributor to the Harlem Renaissance.
- **Edward "Duke" Ellington** – One of America's greatest performers and composers, he wrote more

than 1,000 songs using various musical forms. He received two Grammy Awards and the Medal of Freedom Award.

- **Medgar Evers** – The most prominent civil rights activist in the state of Mississippi until his assassination in June of 1963. His murder intensified the civil rights struggle and was a factor in President John Kennedy asking Congress to enact major Civil Rights legislation.

- **John Hope Franklin** - A prolific author, educator, and historian, he was one of the social scientists that developed the brief for the NAACP's legal argument for the plaintiff's cause in the Brown v. Board of Education case.

- **Althea Gibson** – She was the first African American to compete and win at both the U.S. Open and Wimbledon. She was also the first African American member of the Ladies Professional Golf Association.

- **Berry Gordy, Jr.** – Founder and owner of Motown Records, the most successful African American record company in history, he changed the sound of popular music from rock-n-roll to the distinctive Motown Sound.

- **Fannie Lou Hamer** – A civil rights leader from the South, she led a protest against the Mississippi Democratic Party's all White delegation at the 1964 Democratic Presidential Convention in Atlantic City.

- **Steve Harvey** – Award winning comedian, actor, writer, and nationally syndicated radio talk show host who has and continues to impact the lives of thousands with his inspirational, motivational and charitable work.

- **Langston Hughes** – One of the most powerful writers of the 20th century, his work was considered the voice of the African American middle class during the Harlem Renaissance of the 1920's and the consciousness of the Black working class during the Civil Rights Movement of the 1960's.

- **Rev. Jesse Jackson** – A charismatic civil rights leader that made serious bids to become President of the United States in 1984 and 1988. He currently leads the National Rainbow Coalition to address economic injustice and human rights in America and abroad.

- **John H. Johnson** – Publisher of Ebony and Jet Magazines for more than 50 years, he has provided African Americans with news events of interest along with positive role models and stories of Black success.

- **Michael Jordan** – Four-time National Basketball Association Most Valuable Player, a four time NBA Finals MVP, a two time NBA All-Star Game MVP along with Rookie of the Year, Defensive Player of the Year, two Olympic gold medals and five NBA Championships define him as the greatest basketball player of all time.

- **Tom Joyner** - Founder of the Tom Joyner Foundation, BlackAmericaWeb.com, and host of the nationally syndicated Tom Joyner Morning Show, Tom Joyner Sr., is considered one of the most influential, inspirational, and dynamic personalities in America.

- **Maulana Karenga** – Author, scholar and educator, he created the Kwanzaa cultural holiday for people of African American descent in 1966.

- **Martin Luther King, Jr.** – The most outstanding and prominent civil rights leader of the 1960's. His non-violent approach to civil protest led to voting rights for African Americans and an end to legal employment discrimination and segregation of public facilities. He won a Nobel Peace Prize and his birthday is a national holiday.

- **Spike Lee** – Maker of critically acclaimed and awarded films. His movies are often considered controversial in the way they depict Black life and culture accurately and without stereotypes.

- **Joe Louis** – Best known for being Heavyweight Boxing Champion during the Depression and World War II, he blazed a trail and created opportunities for African Americans in a variety of professional sports, entertainment and business.

- **Thurgood Marshall** – America's first African-American Supreme Court Justice was also the NAACP's Legal Defense and Education Fund special counsel. In that role he had 29 successful winning arguments before the Supreme Court, a record that remains unmatched.

- **Toni Morrison** – A Pulitzer Prize and Nobel Prize winning author, Toni Morrison is also the first African American woman writer to hold a named chair at an Ivy League University.
- **Robert Moses** – A Field Secretary for the Mississippi Student Nonviolent Coordinating Committee, he opened "Freedom Schools" to teach voter registration and community action strategies, held mock elections, and challenged the state's segregated slate of Democratic Convention delegates.
- **Elijah Muhammad** – exposed millions of African Americans to the Islamic faith. He led the Nation of Islam in a separatist movement that stressed the ability of African Americans to control and determine their own destiny through self-reliance.
- **Jesse Owens** – Winner of four Olympic Gold Medals in the 1936 Olympic Games, he carried the pride of the entire nation on his shoulders as he competed, won, and crushed the myth of Aryan superiority. It wouldn't be until twenty years later that America would show appreciation for his accomplishments.
- **Rosa Parks** – She refused to relinquish her bus seat to a White passenger and sparked a movement against segregation in Montgomery, Alabama. That action is recognized today as the launch and kickoff, and she is named the "Mother of the Civil Rights Movement."
- **Sidney Poitier** – A film and stage actor, he is a winner of the American Film Institute's "Lifetime

Achievement Award." Poitier is also the first African American to win a Best Actor Oscar.

- **Adam Clayton Powell** – The first Black Congressman from the northeastern United States and only the fourth Black Representative in the 20th century. He pushed legislation to desegregate the military and public facilities, and to end hiring discrimination.
- **Colin Powell** – The first African American Chairman of the Joint Chiefs of Staff, and the first Black to be National Security Advisor. General Powell led our nation's military through Operation Desert Storm. He is also a bestselling author since the release of his autobiography.
- **A. Philip Randolph** – A trade union organizer, he established the first successful Black Trade Union and led protests to desegregate the military and defense industry. He pioneered the use of nonviolent protest to benefit African Americans.
- **Paul Robeson** – A tremendous singer, actor and noted scholar. His career was stalled because of his efforts as a Human Rights Activist. His passport was restricted by the State Department for 5 years, and he was virtually "black listed" as a performer within the entertainment industry.
- **Jackie Robinson** – The first Black Major League Baseball player and the first African American elected to the Baseball Hall of Fame. He also was active in the Civil Rights Movement to end discrimination and establish economic equality. He

opened Freedom National Bank in Harlem to help finance African American entrepreneurs.

- **Mabel Staupers** – President of the National Association of Colored Graduate Nurses she fought and won for the reverse of the Army and Navy Nurse Corps declaration that they would not accept Black nurses. For her work to integrate nurses into the military, Staupers was awarded the NAACP Spingarn Medal.

- **William Grant Still** – The first African American classical composer to have his symphonic work performed by a major American Orchestra and Opera Company, and the first Black to conduct a major Orchestra in the South.

- **Susan L. Taylor** – Author, inspirational speaker, and Editor-In-Chief of Essence Magazine she has become a leading role model, mentor, and inspiration for Black entrepreneurs and philanthropists. She received the Women in Communications Matrix Award after launching a nationally syndicated television magazine show.

- **Alice Walker** – Her book, *The Color Purple,* which focuses on the impact of domestic violence and racism on three generations of Blacks, has earned her a Pulitzer Prize and American Book Award. The book has been developed into a movie which received 11 Academy Awards.

- **Oprah Winfrey** – Actress, producer, television talk show host, recipient of the Peabody Award, and businesswoman, she has inspired millions to increase their self-esteem and self-reliance. Her philanthropic efforts include a $1 million donation to Morehouse College and opening a school for girls in South Africa.

- **Malcolm X** – As a leader of and spokesman for the Nation of Islam he preached that self-reliance, racial pride and self-determination were necessary for African Americans to gain political and economic power. His fiery oratory caused pause and contemplation in the entire nation during the Civil Rights Movement, as he presented the theory of "By Any Means Necessary" as an effective alternative to nonviolent protest.

- **Whitney Young** – Past Executive Director of the Urban League, he grew the organization from an annual budget of $250,000 and 34 staff to $3,500,000 and 200 staff in six years. A skillful author, his book, *Beyond Racism: Building an Open Society*, describes how the Black Power era could help move the nation toward a more democratic society.

One of the thought provoking aspects that I found with each of the individuals that I reflected on was that they lived and made their significant contribution during my lifetime. In fact many were still alive and making more significant contributions. That fact caused me to ask myself the question, had I lived up to my full potential? Had I given to my family, my people, and society, everything that I had to offer? Had I been the best me that I could be? Had I fulfilled Rosie's long time wish for me to "be somebody?" The answer was not yes, but it also wasn't no. It was a resounding, I tried! I could accept the answer; I tried. It meant that through it all I had given my best, but I felt that I could give more.

Another question that I pondered is, had I done anything that could be considered great. Obviously that leads to the definition of the term great. Not allowing myself to get caught up in a philosophical and ideological mental debate, I settled on the definition that great equals an action that results in a positive impact on those affected. Based on that criterion I had done "great things," but in most instances none of those "great things" would make me famous. Once again I could accept the results to my self-evaluation. I remembered a witticism quoted to me during my pledge experience into Omega Psi Phi Fraternity, "Not all great men are Omegas, but all Omegas are great men." I rephrased the quote to; "Not all men can do great things that become famous, but all men can do great things."

I also spent time thinking about how close of an encounter with death I had survived. I felt that at the time of the heart attack, my life was once again in complete control of God's Saving Grace. Just as Grace had intervened on that fall day when I and my brothers stood helpless on the steps of the city court house, God's Saving Grace was there as I lay on the hospital emergency room table. Once again I felt as if God had looked down and saw that one of His special children was in desperate need and responded with aid and comfort. It was more than apparent to me that God had a plan for my life and that it was not time for my work here on earth to end. One cannot have a more realistic and intimate experience with God than to personally encounter the glorious power of His Saving Grace. The wonderful essence of God's love motivated me to commit that I would do all in my power to live and work to discover and fulfill God's purpose for me, whatever that might ultimately be.

On more than one occasion as I walked, I shouted, jumped up and down, pumped my fist in the air and became filled with joy and happiness at the fact that I had survived. I love life and being alive. I took on a new appreciation for the small things, like the sound of a bird calling to another, or to see a squirrel scurrying across the lawn and up the trunk of a tree. I thought of others that had not been so fortunate. Barry White, the man with the velvet voice; Maynard Jackson, the first Black mayor of Atlanta; Gregory Peck, the Oscar winning actor; David Brinkley, the television news journalist; Robert Stack, the actor; David Bloom, the television newscaster; Maurice Gibbs, the song writer and singer in the rock n' roll band the Bee Gees; were just a few of the celebrity and notable people that had all fallen victim earlier in the year, to heart attacks and associated illnesses like high blood pressure and diabetes. I said prayers of thanksgiving and praise to God for his Mercy and Saving Grace. **Revelations 5:13, And every creature which is in heaven, and on the earth, and under the earth, and such as are in the sea, and all that are in them, heard I saying, Blessing, and honour, and glory, and power, be unto him that sitteth upon the throne, and unto the Lamb for ever and ever.**

Chapter 27

Cardio rehabilitation lasted six months. Barbara took care of my every need. Special no-salt meals with fruits and vegetables were one of her top priorities. Mrs. Arbuckle felt that my road to good health was down a totally new path than the one I had traveled when it came to diet. She spent so much time and put so much effort into my recovery, that she needed a recovery herself. Not just from the work but from the stress that she had endured during the entire event. The emotional toll and impact that I saw her live through could have only been experienced by someone that truly and deeply loved me. I witnessed her feeling my pain, and suffering with me. I am so grateful to her for everything and I will always love her. We took a trip to San Diego, California and Tijuana, Mexico to relax, celebrate, and visit with my Omega brother Michael Dorsey and his wonderful wife Lisa, along with their sons.

I returned to my job at Ford doing half days for three weeks and then fulltime. I returned with the self-determination to be a kinder, gentler person. I committed to myself to be easier and more pleasant to deal with. In the cutthroat, backstabbing, world of corporate life, the meek and humble approach can be difficult to maintain and even more challenging to prosper and thrive under. Time and time again I had to be prayerful, thoughtful and calculated in responses and actions to maintain the commitment.

While at work I mainly focused on a six sigma project to develop environmentally sustainable packaging with one of my coworkers, David Shepps. David is a brilliant statistician with tremendous analytical and engineering design skills. Although his demeanor is short, abrupt, and no nonsense, he is also genuinely a nice guy that is a loving husband and father. At the time we were coupled together as a team, many thought that we would fail because our personalities would clash. My new approach to dealing with issues and people helped me develop a good working relationship and ultimately a close friendship with David. The new approach also started to be very helpful in achieving the collaborations and alliances we needed to accomplish the goals of our team. In fact the results were phenomenal, the groups and individuals that in the past had been the most intense and severe road-blocks, were becoming our greatest supporters. Our project achieved acclaim and accolades throughout the company, the industry, and the academic world. I and the team were invited to present our work to various groups within the company and at industry workshops and seminars. We were noted in industry journals and presented a paper on our patent pending work at Georgia Tech University.

Celebrating 25 years as an employee of Ford Motor Company

On the community service front I continued my work with the Head Start program but stepped down from the taxing role of Board Chairman. I also continued work with the Michigan Neighborhood Partnership and took on the responsibility of Board Chairman at the personal request of the founder, Rev. Eddie Edwards. When he originally asked me to accept the position I declined telling Rev. Edwards that I didn't want to accept any new major responsibility because of my recent heart attack and not wanting to overdo it. He explained to me that he had prayed about it and felt that I would be the best person to take his vision forward and ask that I consider the notion for a month. The board election was five weeks away and I could think about it for a while and he'd have time to find an alternative if I did not accept. Two weeks later Rev. Edwards passed away. I felt compelled to accept the position and do my very best to move his vision forward. I would later discover that my decision was part of a divine plan to achieve the goal of launching a community service program for a special group in need.

Although my service and activity plate was full I still didn't feel as if I was answering the call and doing the service that God wanted me to do. Then one evening while browsing the newspaper Barbara saw a small ad requesting individuals to apply for open positions on the State of Michigan Citizen's Foster Care Review Board. As soon as she saw the ad she knew that I should apply and encouraged me to do so. The application process called for the applicant to provide a resume and write a letter indicating why they wanted to participate. In my letter I wrote that I had been a foster child and knew firsthand what the experience is like. I stated that I had been blessed and fortunate that my experience and the eventual results were a shining example of what the system was designed to yield, and that I may be able to provide some input that could enhance the current system. In my heart I knew that this was the direction that God wanted me to go. I was approved and appointed by Governor Jennifer Granholm to be a member of the State of Michigan Citizen's Foster Care Review Board.

The mission of the Foster Care Review Board is to use citizen volunteers to review and evaluate permanency planning processes and outcomes for children and families in the Michigan foster care system. Based on the findings from reviewed cases the board presses for improvements in the system in areas of child safety, timely permanency, and family and child well-being. I learned that the board is viewed and valued by the courts, the Department of Human Services, private child-placing agencies, the legislature, and the good people of Michigan as a major source of credible information on the performance of the child welfare system in Michigan. I also discovered that the information provided by the board was used to shape public policy and promote public awareness regarding the foster care system. The board is made up of private citizens that meet once a month to review the cases of abused or neglected children in foster care. The central focus of the reviews is to assess plans for permanency and care of children in foster care.

Most of my time spent working with the Foster Care Review Board was a learning experience. I learned that while there were core issues that progress had been made on, there are four issues that remain in fundamental form and require continuous improvement. They are:

Case Service Plans for reuniting families;
- Parents don't always have input into the Case Service Plan.
- Case Service Plans aren't always written with sufficient specificity so that parents are clear about expectations.

Caseloads and Staff Turnover;
- There is a high turnover rate of foster care workers. Turnovers can cause delays in implementation of service plans and court hearings, and adds stress to workers who must handle additional workload until new people are hired and trained.

- There is a significant difference in the salary and benefits between private agency foster care workers and DHS employees.

Permanent Wards (Permanent wards are children in foster care after parental rights have been terminated, with no finalized permanency plan.);

- The number of permanent wards in the state of Michigan has risen steadily since 1997 from 3,800 to over 6,200 in 2004.
- It is much more difficult to find adoptive homes, or establish other permanency plans, for older children in the foster care system.

Mental Health, Substance Abuse, and Domestic Violence;

- The most prevalent barriers to permanency for temporary wards are those related to parental issues. Among the parental issues, three of the most challenging are concerns related to substance abuse, mental health and domestic violence.
- Successful treatment of substance abuse does not always happen within the time frame that the courts and the child welfare system have established for child abuse or neglect cases.
- Timely and high quality services are not consistently available throughout the State to address substance abuse and mental health issues.
- Victims of domestic violence often confront difficult challenges as they weigh options for their own safety and seek to protect their children.

Over time we developed recommendations to address the core issues. We also reviewed randomly selected and requested cases of children in foster care for the purpose of determining if the court and agencies responsible for developing and carrying out a permanency plan are effective and efficient doing it. We also heard appeals from foster parents that disagreed with the movement of a ward from their home. The reviews were conducted in two stages. The first stage involved reading the written material detailing the reason for out of home placement and the agency's plan for services to the child and family. The second stage is an in-person interview with interested parties in the case, such as the caseworker, the biological parents, the foster parents and, if appropriate, the child.

My work with the Foster Care Review Board was one of the most emotional endeavors I had ever undertaken. To read the stories and see the faces of those that had been abused or neglected was so heart wrenching. I decided that I could not personally make a positive impact on all the issues or the related systemic issues of foster care, so I had to focus on one small element that would have the biggest impact. I decided that I would focus on the issue of "aging out of the system."

One of the biggest fears that I dealt with as a young adult emerging from the system was a lack of support when no one was legally required to do so. I was afraid to be totally on my own, all alone in the world with no one to turn to. I discovered that most of my friends were too, even though they didn't want to admit it, and most of them had the benefit of a family support network. Fortunately for me there was the structure and support system of college and the continued support of the Yearbys. One can only imagine the feeling of solitude, hopelessness, fear, and emptiness a young person must feel when they realize that on their eighteenth birthday, no one has to care about them except for the individual having the realization. Over night, they have no income, no home, no family, not even the foster family that was created for them. They become totally responsible to provide for themselves the means to live independently. Literally hundreds of children have that experience annually because the system could not develop a permanency plan.

I began highlighting the issue of "aging out of the foster care system" with my colleagues and fellow board members of the Michigan Neighborhood Partnership. It was not long before we developed a program and found funding to address the issue. Our program was designed to provide life skills training to manage independent living. We were able to collaborate with other programs like the Jim Casey Youth Opportunities Initiatives to develop a broader system of support for children aging out of the foster care system with financial support for costs related to establishing independent living. In addition, in November of 2004 the Michigan State Supreme Court launched the Children's Community Service Network. That program matched community volunteers with children in the foster care system with an emphasis on providing mentoring and support for older children.

The Department of Labor and Economic Growth and The Department of Human Services received a Foster Youth Demonstration Grant to provide comprehensive services to youth that age out of the child welfare system. The Department of Human Services also received technical assistance from the National Resource Center on Youth Development to improve policy and practice for youth exiting the system. While these steps are not the total solution, the issue is being addressed and some progress made. While my efforts were subtle and behind the scenes, the impact could surely be felt by those that needed it most. **James 1:27, Pure religion and undefiled before God and the Father is this. To visit the fatherless and widows in their affliction, and to keep himself unspotted from the world. Matthew 25:35, For I was hungry, and ye gave me meat, I was thirsty, and ye gave me drink: I was a stranger, and ye took me in; v.40, And the King shall answer and say unto them, Verily I say unto you, Inasmuch as ye have done it unto one of the least of these my brethren, ye have done it unto me. Hebrews 6:10, For God is not unrighteous to forget your work and labour of love, which ye have sewed toward his name, in that ye have ministered to the saints, and do minister.**

Chapter 28

By early 2007 life in the world of the Arbuckle family was as normal as could be expected for our family. Marseille, Jr. was off in college at the University of Michigan in Ann Arbor, Michigan. While it's only 25 miles from our house, it seemed as if he was a world away. Our daughter Jamillah and her family had moved to East Lansing, Michigan. My son-in-law Theo had obtained a position with the staff of Michigan State University so he moved his family closer to his job, which was a very sensible thing to do. Barbara and I took the 60 miles or so drive to visit them regularly so we could keep ourselves involved in the lives of our two youngest and wonderful grandsons Jonah and Noah. We also enjoyed going to various events around town although we had slowed our pace of attending formal functions and banquets a considerable amount. The lifestyle of empty nesters suited us just fine.

One of the results of life after surviving a massive heart attack for me was to become much more health conscience and practice heart healthy living. A key aspect of that is to maintain a good relationship with your physician and closely monitor your system to make sure everything is in good condition. The first key step to achieving my heart healthy life style goal was to establish a good relationship with my doctor. I needed my doctor to be someone that I could feel comfortable with asking questions and sharing the intricate details of my physical being with. A year after I suffered the heart attack my primary care physician left the healthcare insurance system that I was a part of, so I had to select a new one. I used this as an opportunity to find a doctor that I could interface with on a close level, as well as one that I had extremely high confidence in as being an outstanding doctor. I selected Dr. Roderick Walker to become my primary care physician. Roderick is a member of Omega Psi Phi, as I am, and he graduated from the University of Michigan, a Big Ten Conference school as I had done. Dr. Walker also has an outstanding academic record at the University of Michigan Medical School and a proven track record of success with hundreds of healthy, happy patients; what more could I ask for.

Along with maintaining a healthy diet and regular exercise I feel a vital part of healthy living is to visit the doctor on a regular basis, which I had only done if I had a specific ailment in the past. Dr. Walker and I developed a quarterly appointment schedule with various tests and checks for my heart, blood pressure and cardio related issues. Just prior to my spring 2007 doctor's visit, Barbara mentioned that I should have a prostate exam. I knew that I had reached the age which requires regular prostate screening, but because I dislike the awkwardness and discomfort of the infamous "DRE" (digital rectal examination), I avoided it. During my visit I mentioned to Roderick that I probably needed to have my prostate checked but that I wanted to do it at the next visit, "I'm not in the mood for it today so put it in the notes so that I don't forget at the next examination," I said and laughed. "Marsialle I can get a blood sample and check your PSA level today," Dr. Walker responded. He then said with a smirk and half chuckle, "Hey frat, I don't have any more desire to give you a DRE than you have to get one. I'll call you in a couple of days and give you the results. Be sure to stop at the lab on your way out and let the lab technician draw some blood."

I received a call two days later from Dr. Walker. He said, "Marsialle your PSA level or prostate-specific antigen in the blood should be less than 4 nanograms per milliliter. Your PSA level is at 4.2. Now don't get excited, it could have been high on the day and at the time that the blood sample was taken for any number of reasons. If you had sex the night before there is a good chance that the PSA level will be elevated. What we'll do is check it again during your next scheduled appointment in the summer." The next three months went by quickly, and I had done as suggested, I didn't get excited, in fact I forgot all about it.

My next doctor's appointment was scheduled for mid-June of the year. Dr. Walker didn't mention my prostate during the examination until the end of the visit when he reminded me to stop at the lab on the way out to provide a blood sample so he could take another look at my PSA level. I did as requested and went along home. Two days later the phone rang at my office. It was Dr. Walker, "Marsialle, hello this Dr. Walker, I have the results of your PSA test, do you have time to stop by the office this afternoon?" "Sure, I can be there around five or five thirty if that's not too late," I said. "I believe that will be fine but let me transfer you to the receptionist and she'll make sure," he replied. "Hey Roderick, what's up frat?" I asked. "Relax, I don't think it's a big deal, but we need to discuss it. I'll see you later this afternoon," with that I was transferred to the receptionist.

During my visit with Roderick that afternoon he explained that my PSA level had risen higher since the last check and that he was concerned. He felt that I should visit an urologist that he would recommend. That doctor would do a DRE and most likely a biopsy as well. He explained that a biopsy is a procedure in which the doctor uses trans-rectal ultrasound to view and guide a needle into the prostate to take multiple small samples of tissue. These tissues are then examined under a microscope for the presence of cancer. Dr. Walker explained that a biopsy is the only way to confirm or diagnose the presence of prostate cancer. At the end of our discussion I took the card that had the name and number of the urologist written on it and went home to tell Barbara.

When I shared my situation with Barbara she was pretty shaken up. That actually was a good thing and very helpful to me because my focus became comforting and providing assurance to her that everything would be alright. My focus became so directed at her that I didn't focus on feeling sorry for myself. The assurance that I was giving her was reassurance for me. I told her that God had taken care of me all of my life. I said to her that my very existence is a miracle and that God hadn't brought me this far to abandon me. We prayed together for God to show us mercy and allow us to avoid cancer. We also prayer for the strength of faith and the courage to face and deal with cancer if that was our burden to bear.

Later that evening and for the next several weeks, Barbara and I did an exhausting amount of research on the various approaches to treatment for prostate cancer. If it was determined that I did have prostate cancer we were going to be fully knowledgeable about the disease and various approaches to treatment including the most state-of-the-art. I visited the urologist and had the biopsy performed, which was a very unpleasant experience, and that's all I have to say about that. The results were extremely slow in coming which caused Barbara and me a great deal of stress and frustration. I called after the second week and pressed for the results. The situation was intensified by the fact that the initial response that I received back was that things looked clear. The next day while driving along I-94 on a return business trip my cell phone rang, it was the urologist's office calling with an urgent request for me to stop by their office immediately. I drove directly there, not thinking for the next hour and a half about what the most probable reason was for my needing to be seen in person by the urologist.

When I arrived I was taken into a small consultation room, and after a few moments the door opened and the urologist entered. He had a booklet and several documents in his hand. He smiled and asked me how I was feeling as he pulled a stool on rollers from under a counter on the side of the room and sat on it. His face continued to maintain the slight hint of a smile as he made eye contact and began to speak in a matter-of-fact monotone voice. "Mr. Arbuckle the first several slides from your biopsy were negative for tumors but the remaining slides reflect malignant or cancerous tumor cells on one side of your prostate. That is why we usually wait until all the samples have been thoroughly analyzed before sharing the results. Since you had called we gave you the preliminary partial findings which suggested that everything was clear. After we completed the analysis we made the discovery." The doctor paused as I took a breath in an attempt to absorb everything that was being said. He continued, "Mr. Arbuckle we believe that your TNM stage is T1c which means that tumor cells were identified during a needle biopsy performed to investigate PSA elevation." Excuse me I interrupted, "What is TNM?" "Tumor, Node, Metastases," he replied, "T refers to the size of the tumor, N describes the extent of regional lymph node involvement and M refers to the presence or absence of metastases or cancer that has spread into the bones. We think that you're at T1c which is one of the earliest stages of the disease. We'll need to do some extensive tests including a MRI or full body scan to confirm what we believe. Once we've done that we can decide on your treatment plan."

Somewhat dazed and overwhelmed I ask the urologist what was the next step going to be. He told me the list of tests that I needed to have conducted and where to get them done. As we rose from our seats, he placed his hand on my shoulder and said, "Mr. Arbuckle prostate cancer is one of the most common forms of cancer and with early detection one of the most curable. Most men don't die from prostate cancer but with it. 92% of all men diagnosed with prostate cancer live 10 or more years and over 60% survive beyond 15 years." While I knew that the doctor was well intentioned in his last comments, they didn't have their intended effect. My feeling was that prostate cancer was an older man's disease. To hear that you have another 10 or 15 years to live has got to sound a lot better to a 70 or 75 year old man than it does to a 49 year old. I looked at the doctor and said thank you as I walked through the door and headed to my car.

As I rode home I thought to myself that I was about to face a challenge that many other men had faced. I knew two fraternity brothers very well, that had recently survived prostate cancer. One was my mentor, Tyrone Havard, for whom I had been at the hospital and at his home to visit during his recovery. The other was David Mitchell, a fellow boater that docks his vessel just a few slips from mine. I had watched them both during their battle and recovery and both were doing fine. David in particular seemed to have been minimally affected by the surgery and never missed a beat. I would make it a point to talk with him and get his input and advice on dealing with prostate cancer. I also decided that I would be deeply involved with the treatment planning since there were several options.

Informing Barbara of the news was difficult. I knew that she would be upset which I didn't want. I also knew that I had to tell her and her being upset couldn't be avoided. I tried to share the news in the most positive way possible. To my surprise Barbara was very consoling and supportive of me. To her the most important issue was that we were totally knowledgeable about all of the options and approaches available so that we selected the optimal approach to treatment and dealing with my cancer. I needed her strength and support and it was there. In the depths of my mind I thought of the horrible way cancer can ravish a person. I remembered the suffering that James Yearby, my foster dad Walter's older brother, endured. I was just 4 or

5 years old during the time of his illness. I remembered going to his home in Chicago with Walter and Rosie and hearing his coughing and hacking, moans, and groans come from behind the partially closed door of the bedroom in his flat on Cottage Grove Avenue. I thought of people I had seen that had lost weight to the point of frailty. Their hair fallen out and their skin darkened to a point where they were barely recognizable as a result of chemotherapy. I didn't want to have to deal with those things but I knew that I would have to if that is what it would take to battle cancer and win.

I went about the business of taking the various blood tests, x-rays, and the MRI or full body scan. It took several weeks to complete all of the appointments and get the results. During that time Barbara and I became experts on prostate cancers and the various forms of treatment available. We decided that the best form of treatment for me would be a radical prostatectomy performed via robotic surgery. The approach would be minimally invasive, thereby requiring the least amount of recovery time. The approach also offered one of the highest rates of total removal of the cancer from my body. My only concern would be the impact of surgery on my blood pressure which is high but controlled and my heart which is less than 100% functional as a result of the heart attack.

By the time I was to meet with the urologist, Barbara and I had developed a written version of my treatment plan. We had a list of questions that I would ask and we had identified Dr. Mani Menon at the Vatikuti Urology Institute of Henry Ford Health Systems to conduct the procedure at Henry Ford Hospital. During our research we had learned of Dr. Menon and his pioneering work done in the field of robotic prostate surgery. We were surprised and delighted to discover that right in our metropolitan area, the most state-of-the-art technology and one of the leading doctors in the field was available. We learned that people all over the world travel to Detroit for treatment by Dr. Menon and his team at the institute, including a couple of very high ranking federal government officials.

The time of the appointment was in the middle of the day. Barbara and I agreed to meet at the doctor's office in separate cars, so we could minimize the amount of time we would miss from work. She had just begun a new job and didn't need to be out of the office. Once again, when I arrived at the urologist office I was taken into the same small consultation room, this time Barbara was at my side. Barbara sat on the same stool as I had before and I stood as we waited for the doctor to enter. This time after the knock on the door a different doctor entered the room prior to the urologist that we were expecting to see. It was a woman wearing a white doctor's smock, she was small in stature and had her hair pulled back into a bun. She appeared to be of Indian descent. As I looked at the name badge I determined that my assumption was correct by the name, but what stood out more was the title, Vascular Surgeon. Why would a vascular surgeon be coming into the consultation room? Before I could ponder the thought any further, the usual urologist stepped through the door and began speaking. Once again making eye contact and in the same monotone and matter-of-fact voice he said, "Hello Mr. Arbuckle, this doctor is a vascular surgeon," pointing to the woman, "She'll be observing and may take part in the discussion." I nodded and pointed toward Barbara with an open hand and said, "This is my wife Barbara." The doctor smiled at her and nodded his head at her a couple of times quickly as he pulled the second stool from under the counter and sat on it. The tension seemed to mount as a moment or two passed with no one speaking. "Well I'm ready to get down to it with my treatment plan but first I have a couple of questions," I said in a "full-of-pep" tone attempting to reflect the fact that I would be taking control and leading our discussion. I looked down and opened the notebook that I had brought along with me that was filled with questions and all the data and facts that Barbara and I had assembled over the past few weeks and days. As I looked up I noticed the urologist's hand going up and out in the halt, don't go any further motion. I stopped what I was about to say in the middle of a word. "Uh, Mr. Arbuckle," the doctor said in a lower tone than he had ever used before, "We can't discuss your prostate cancer treatment plan right now, because we've discovered that you have an issue more serious than cancer."

An issue more serious than cancer, I thought to myself. Barbara and I looked at each other in shock but didn't or couldn't speak. While I was hoping for the doctor to say that the test results indicated that the cancer had not spread and was isolated to my prostate, I had prepared myself for what I thought could be the worst news and that being the cancer had spread to my lymph nodes or into my pelvis and bone marrow. What could be more serious than cancer?

I had already had a heart attack, high blood pressure and survived a head on car collision and a motorcycle crash, broken bones and pneumonia. I had driven myself to the facility and walked in the door under my own power, what could I possibly have that's more serious than cancer?

Before I could form my mouth to ask the question the doctor spoke and broke the silence, "While reviewing the MRI, it was detected that you have an abdominal aortic aneurysm or what we commonly refer to as a triple A. It has reached a size of 5.2cm, which is considered at a critical stage or size." I was shocked and didn't know exactly what to say. The doctor went on to explain that an aneurysm is a weakening of the walls of an artery or vein so that it balloons out. At a certain point the breached area can burst. He said that aneurysms can form anywhere in the blood vessels, but are found most commonly in the blood vessels of the brain and in the aorta, the main vessel for arterial blood. He said that if the aneurysm that was in my abdomen or stomach were to rupture, the odds were that I would bleed to death before surgery to repair it could be started. Therefore it was critical that I get it addressed almost immediately. It was his opinion that I needed to get it handled before addressing the cancer issue.

The urologist went on to tell me that the cancer in my prostate was in the very early stage and that it was on the left side of my prostate. The tumors appeared to be isolated to that area. He said that I had some time to deal with the prostate issues, especially since I hadn't begun experiencing any symptoms, but that I didn't want to put it off too long because time would allow the tumors to grow and the cancer to progress. On the other hand he felt that the size of the aneurysm required immediate attention and that the vascular surgeon could provide further consultation on the matter. At that point I asked the doctor, "How much time do you feel that I have before my aorta will rupture?" The two doctors looked at each other and the vascular surgeon spoke, "It is very difficult to say, I've seen aneurysms expand to 7cm or even 8cm, but I also know of ruptures at 6cm and 6.5cm." Next I asked the million dollar question, "Doctor, can this problem be fixed?" "Yes," the vascular surgeon replied quickly with a slight and brief smile that transformed into a look of extreme seriousness as she explained in detail the major surgery that would be required to repair the aneurysm. She explained that I would get an incision down the front of my body from the bottom of my chest to the tip of my pubic area and be stretched open. The blood to both the lower half an upper half of my body would be clamped off to isolate the section of aorta that contains the aneurysm. The artery would be sliced open and a tube graft inserted to act as a bridge for the blood flow. The artery would then be sutured around the graft and a wrapping put around that. She said the graft is made of synthetic material that has been shown to be very safe. Everything would be then put back into place and the clamps removed. The doctor said that barring the movement of any plaque from the walls of my blood vessels to my heart when the rush of blood flows through after removal of the clamps, the surgery would be successful.

"This operation is safe. There are, however, several possible risks and complications, which are unlikely, but possible," the doctor said in a sympathetic tone. She told me that in reviewing my medical history, she learned that I was a heart attack survivor, and that my hypertension and heart disease may cause some issues during the surgery. She said that because of the risks associated with general anesthesia, a cardiologist would need to be a part of the surgical team and consult with the anesthesiologist.

I asked if there were any other risks. The doctor said that there are some risks that would be associated with any type of surgery like infection, either deep or skin level. If a deep infection were to occur, the graft may need to be taken out and replaced. Bleeding, either during or after the operation, may require blood transfusions or another operation. The vascular surgeon told us that complications could include sexual dysfunction. The nerves that control erection and ejaculation may be closely attached to the aneurysm and may be divided or damaged during the operation. I asked was there anything I could or should start or stop doing, which would help matters. I was told no heavy lifting or straining, especially nothing exceeding 35 pounds.

"Well, you know," I said, "I think I'm going to go home right now and think everything over and then I'll get back with you." "Alright, Mr. Arbuckle, I understand," the urologist replied. I was told that I could make an appointment with the vascular surgeon at the desk on the way out. "I know all this is a bit overwhelming right now," the doctor said as I reached for the door knob. "You're right about that," I responded. "Well consider this Mr. Arbuckle; you're actually one very fortunate person, or a lucky man, or whatever you want to call it. You see, most people never find out that they have a triple A, their family finds out that's what they died from."

Chapter 29

My drive home from the urologist's office is like a blur. I can't remember the route I took or the landmarks that I passed. I just remember hearing those eight words over and over again; you have an issue more serious than cancer. That phrase would change my life forever. It would impact my relationships, my spiritual focus, my finances, my career, and my priorities in life. I tried to make sense of it all. It seemed as if things in my life had shifted to an immediate fast forward. Suddenly things that I had put on the back burner took on extreme urgency, because this could be it.

Only once before had I faced the possibility that I might not make it. Even during the heart attack I never thought that I wouldn't prevail. This time however the reality of the possible end of my existence was looking me in the face and I was looking back at it and there was nothing to obstruct my view. The surgery itself seemed so complex and the added issues of high blood pressure and a partially functional heart put the odds against me. If things go wrong, what happens to Barbara?

If things don't go right what happens to Marseille's college? If, my heart can't take the strain, what happens then? If, there is an infection, what will they do? If the surgery goes fine, what will I do about the cancer?

The word "if," became a very big word. So I decided to think about "if." The most compelling thing about "if," was that I could use it in a negative approach to my situation or a positive approach. Either way, "if" was still there. I knew in my heart that I would meet the situation head on, and mentally approach everything in this situation as a fight. I perform my best when I feel I'm fighting, so I needed to fight this situation. Then I thought of the poem "If" by Rudyard Kipling that I had been required to memorize during the pledge program into Omega Psi Phi Fraternity.

> If you can keep your head when all about you
> Are losing theirs and blaming it on you,
> If you can trust yourself when all men doubt you,
> But make allowances for their doubting too;
> If you can wait and not be tired by waiting,
> Or being lied about, don't deal in lies,
> Or being hated, don't give way to hating,
> And yet don't look too good, nor talk too wise;
>
> If you can dream – and not make dreams your master;
> If you can think – and not make thoughts your aim;
> If you can meet with Triumph and Disaster
> And treat those two impostors just the same;
> If you can bear to hear the truth you've spoken

Twisted by knaves to make a trap for fools,
Or watch the things you gave your life to, broken,
And stoop and build 'em up with worn-out tools;

If you can make one heap of all your winnings
And risk it on one turn of pitch-in-toss
And lose, and start again at your beginnings
And never breathe a word about your loss;
If you can force your heart and nerve and sinew
To serve your turn long after they are gone
And so hold on when there is nothing in you
Except the will which says to them, "Hold On"

If you can talk with crowds and keep your virtue,
'Or walk with kings – nor lose the common touch.
If neither foes, nor loving friends can hurt you
If all men count with you but non too much
If you can fill the unforgiving minute
With sixty seconds worth of distance run.
Yours is the earth and everything that's in it.
And – which is more - you'll be a man my son!

The contents of Mr. Kipling's poem helped to lend perspective to my thinking. I had to meet the challenge of many of the "ifs", which he had identified. Yet there seemed to be another "if", an "if" that I couldn't focus on, the "if" that only God had the knowledge and control of and I had to leave that to him. I had to focus on the positive aspects and possibilities attached to "if". God had protected me through my entire life as one of His special children and I knew this time the only difference would be the magnitude of this miracle. **Romans 8:18, For I reckon that the sufferings of this present time are not worthy to be compared with the glory which shall be revealed in us.**

When I reviewed the status of things with Barbara that evening I tried to be as upbeat as possible but we both knew the seriousness of my illnesses. The crazy thing about it was that I felt fine. I was feeling absolutely fantastic. I had lost weight and was eating right. I was walking or working out daily and getting to bed early, so I was full of energy and looking better than ever on the outside. Yet on the inside my body was infected with cancer and my internal plumbing was about to explode. We both just held each other that night. I'm sure she was praying and so was I. I went to sleep making the promise that I would fight and reciting the words to the poem "See It Through", by Edgar A. Guest;

> **When you're up against a trouble,**
> **Meet it squarely, face to face;**
> **Lift your chin and set your shoulders,**
> **Plant your feet and take a brace.**
> **When it's vain to try to dodge it,**
> **Do the best that you can do;**
> **You may fail, but you may conquer,**
> **See it through!**
>
> **Black may be the clouds about you**
> **And your future may seem grim,**
> **But don't let your nerve desert you;**
> **Keep yourself in fighting trim.**
> **If the worst is bound to happen,**

Spite of all that you can do,
Running from it will not save you,
See it through!
Even hope may seem but futile,
When with troubles you're beset,
But remember you are facing
Just what other men have met.
You may fail, but fall still fighting;
Don't give up, whate'er you do;
Eyes front, head high to the finish.
See it through!

The next morning Barbara and I began trying to figure out our next move. I was happy to have a teammate and partner to stand with me in my fight. I was so glad not to have to face this alone. We decided the first step would be to get a second opinion from both another urologist and another vascular surgeon. We figured that the best thing to do would be to continue down the path we had already taken and attempt to get an opinion from Dr. Menon. Although I thought it would be difficult, getting to meet with Dr. Menon was just the matter of a phone call and setting the appointment.

The nurse that made the appointment told me that I would need to provide a copy of the slides from the biopsy and a complete set of my medical records. Since the data was collected at Oakwood Hospital, it would be faster if I went and picked-up a set of everything and hand delivered the materials so nothing would get disconnected or misplaced. I quickly agreed and actually enjoyed getting personally involved at a hands-on level in the process. It gave me the feeling of some small sense of control.

Barbara and I continued to assemble the medical team which we dubbed with the tag "Med-Team Buck." I consulted Dr. Walker and he recommended a vascular surgeon that had an office in the new St. Mary's Cancer Center around the corner from where we live. My visit with him set the tone for the remainder of my journey in the crisis. I decided that I had everything to gain, and just as much to lose. So I wanted all my questions answered fully and clearly to my total satisfaction. I asked the doctor some very frank questions, and to my surprise he was willing to be equally as frank and pointed in his answers.

To both Barbara and my extreme surprise, this doctor felt that I should address the prostate cancer first. His rationale was simple, but made great sense; he felt that the scar tissue from the aneurysm repair surgery would be so severe that it would prevent robotic surgery for the prostate. That would result in a much more serious and invasive form of surgery to address the cancer. The down side to his approach was that both surgeries would need to be performed with a short period of time between the two, and they both needed to be done soon. He said that because I was in relatively good health and not over weight, he felt good about my heart but that he would want a cardiologist to do a stress test and concur prior to any surgery.

I asked the doctor where was the best place to get the vascular surgery done and if he was the best to do it considering my hypertension and cardio issues. He told me that the best vascular surgeons are at the University of Michigan hospital.

He also said that there was one very experienced vascular surgeon at Oakwood Hospital. He said that doctor had done about ten times the number of successful abdominal aortic aneurysm repairs as he. I asked what that number was and he said more than half a dozen, and less than ten. I then asked the doctor to review the film from the MRI with me and show me the aneurysm. The doctor was very detailed and patient in reviewing the slides of the MRI with Barbara and me. He showed us my aorta from different directions and points of view. He showed us what a normal aorta would look like and the large bulge in my aorta. We discussed the steps involved in the surgery, the recovery process, and life after surgery. As we were bringing the visit to a close he echoed the feelings of the previous doctors, I was fortunate to have been diagnosed with prostate cancer, or I probably would not have discovered the "triple A" in time.

That evening as I was saying my prayers I began to say something that I couldn't believe I was thinking or saying, "Thank you Lord for blessing me with prostate cancer." **Romans 8:26-28, Likewise the Spirit also helpeth our infirmities: for we know not what we should pray for as we ought: but the Spirit itself maketh intercession for us with groanings which cannot be uttered. And he that searcheth the hearts knoweth what is the mind of the Spirit, because he maketh intercession for the saints according to the will of God. And we know that all things work together for good to them that love God, to them who are the called according to his promise.**

The after math of my last doctors' visit created more confusion and frustration. I now had two conflicting opinions, one was to deal with the aneurysm first and the other to deal with the cancer first. I hoped that my next visit to a doctor would clarify things some. In the meantime Barbara attempted to setup an appointment for me at University of Michigan hospital. To our shock and dismay we discovered that the HMO we had selected for coverage would not cover visits to the University of Michigan hospital or its clinics. Suddenly there was a new factor involved, insurance, or the bottom line, money. While researching things online Barbara had confirmed the earlier vascular surgeon's claim that the vascular surgery team at the University of Michigan was some of the best and tops in the field. She also confirmed that Dr. James Lulek at Oakwood Hospital was highly acclaimed, and to our pleasant surprise, he had taught at University of Michigan Medical School and Hospital. I thought to myself, "Well if I can't have the best student, then I'll certainly take his teacher."

The more I prayed on the situation and as time passed I began to feel more and more as if this was a journey that God wanted me to take and that he had things well in control. **Romans 8:24-25, For we are saved by hope: but hope that is seen is not hope: what a man seeth, why doth he yet hope for? But if we hope for that we see not, then do we with patience wait for it.** My visit to Dr. Menon was reassuring and solidified the plan of approach that Barbara and I felt would be best. He agreed that the prostate cancer should be addressed first if I wanted to use robotic surgery. He agreed that the prostatectomy was the most practical approach to treatment considering my age and the stage of development of the tumors. He also, like the others, had some concerns regarding my heart but felt that a cardiologist could prescribe medications that would control both my blood pressure and heart rate during surgery. I officially signed Dr. Menon onto "Med-Team Buck." We set the date for my surgery to be October 18, 2007. As I was about to leave his office Dr. Menon made an observation, he said that it was good that I had decided to have the condition of my prostate checked when I did, it allowed me to find out about the presence of cancerous tumor cells in my prostate and to address another very serious health issue. Dr. Menon was the third doctor to tell me that the cancer was a blessing.

The next leg of the journey was to meet with Dr. Lulek. Barbara and I made this visit together. Dr. Lulek has a great bedside manner and was extremely reassuring. He stressed the point that after reviewing all of the film from the MRI, he could repair my aorta. He also agreed that the prostate surgery should be done first and that my hypertension and heart condition would be a concern but he felt that it could be managed. He made sure that he had answered all of our questions and addressed any concerns. Dr. Lulek said that he would need to do my surgery the first week of December because he was leaving the country the following week and would not be returning until February of 2008. He said that he knew it was a short recovery period from the first surgery, but we didn't have the luxury of lots of time. Dr. Lulek also mentioned one thing that we hadn't considered, that was that he would petition the insurance company and determine if they would approve the surgery and get back with us. One of the harsh realities of life in America was facing me, health insurance. This was the second time along this journey that the insurance company had come into play and could be a potential road block.

While we waited to hear back from Dr. Lulek, Barbara and I pressed forward. Our next leg in the journey was to identify and consult with a cardiologist. We both agreed that since I would be getting treatment at both Henry Ford and Oakwood hospitals, it would be best to get a cardiologist that covers both locations. Our research led us to the name Akshay Khandelwal, MD. I made a telephone call and scheduled an appointment. Dr. Khandelwal is a dynamic and charismatic person that inspired me with his energy and enthusiasm. He also started things off on the right foot with a couple of unexpected compliments regarding my weight and the fact that I looked to be in great condition. I had provided him with a set of all of the film, slides, disks, and other materials that had been created along the journey, so that he had a full set of my medical history and records. Dr. Khandelwal said that based on my history and what was coming he was going to make some adjustments to my medication. He wanted to bring my blood pressure and heart rate down more and get total control of my triglycerides and cholesterol. He said that he felt confident that he could have me ready to meet the timing that the procedures were scheduled for. My job would be to follow the dietary rules and take the prescribed medications according to the directions. I agreed and promised to do as instructed. The final member of "Med-Team Buck" was in place and the time to step into the ring was drawing near. The fight was on!

Chapter 30

I spent the last couple of weeks prior to the first surgery contacting friends and family. I also spent lots of time at the marina, sitting on the boat reading the Bible, meditating, and praying. It was difficult to focus at work, my mind constantly drifted to my pending hospital stays and the long term impact that would be the result. I spent hours going over all the possible risks. My abdominal organs like my liver or intestines could be damaged. My kidneys, or bladder, and the tubes that connect them could be injured. There's the rare chance of spinal cord stroke, resulting in paralysis.

With both surgeries I had the issue of general anesthesia. There would be the nausea, vomiting, urinary retention, sore throat and headaches. Also, there loomed the more serious risk for me of heart attack or stroke. With both surgeries I could have blood clots due to inactivity during and after the surgery. Blood clots become dislodged from the leg and go to the lungs where they will cause shortness of breath, chest pain, and possibly death.

Each day I would leave the office and go directly to the marina. When necessary I attended civic meetings to inform the group that I was resigning from my position or office, in order to focus on my health and deal with family and personal matters. I didn't mind stepping down from various positions, and in each case I would make it a point to mention that I was stepping down but not out! I truly believed that I would overcome these health issues and that God had more for me to do in my work and existence here.

I was uplifted and inspired by the outpouring of support that I and the family received from my circle of friends including church members, fraternity and lodge members, all of the organizations that I worked with and most importantly my family. One of the Omega Psi Phi fraternity brothers that reached out to me was Harold Puckett a longtime friend from Gary, Indiana. He had attended Indiana University as I had. He became a member of the fraternity a year before I did, but our hometown connection linked us as friends. When Harold called I was a bit surprised but very appreciative of the call. At first we updated each other on the status of our families, careers, and other pleasantries. Then Harold mentioned the issue of my health and told me that he had faced difficult times with his mother's failing health and ultimately passing away.

Harold told me that during those times his faith in God had increased more than ever. I told him that it was my faith that was providing me with peace of mind during this waiting period. If I didn't have faith in God and His healing power, I would have stressed out over this situation. I also have faith that however things turnout, God has a plan for me and that so far His plan had been nothing less than a series of miracles throughout my life. Some of the miracles were big and visible to everyone, and others have been subtle and only I could feel the power, but the power has been there none the less. After we prayed together over the phone, Harold said that there was some scripture that he wanted me to read. He said that I would find the passage inspiring and powerful, Harold Puckett was right. Harold suggested that I read **2 Kings 20: 1-7, In those days was Hezekiah sick unto death. And the prophet Isaiah the son of Amoz came to him, and said unto him, Thus saith the Lord, Set thine house in order, for thou shalt die, and not live. Then he turned his face to the wall, and prayed unto the Lord saying, I beseech thee, O Lord, remember now how I have walked before thee in truth and with a perfect heart, and have done that which is good in thy sight. And Hezekiah wept sore. And it came to pass afore Isaiah was gone out into the middle court, that the Lord came to him saying, Turn again and tell Hezekiah the captain of my people, Thus saith the Lord, the God of David thy father, I have heard thy prayer, I have seen thy tears; behold I will heal thee: on the third day thou shalt go up unto the house of the Lord. And I will add unto thy days fifteen years: and I will deliver thee and this city out of the hand of the king of Assyria; I will defend this city for my own sake, and for my servant David's sake. And Isaiah said, Take a lump of figs. And they took and laid it on the boil, and he recovered.**

When I called my sister Royletta and informed her of my status, she surprised me by saying that she would be here on the day of the surgery. I was very happy and touched that she wanted to be at my side. My sisters-in-law Beverly and Andrea also decided that they would come and lend their support to me and their sister. Once again I was flattered by the love and caring support. October 18th seemed to arrive in the time that it takes to bat an eye. It was time for the first in a series of miracles to occur.

We all left for the hospital early that morning. When I arrived at the registration area I was surprised to see a member of the church ministerial staff there waiting for me. The Minister prayed with the family and me, and then Barbara and I were escorted to the surgical prep room. I was given the traditional backless gown, shaved (I asked for a bikini cut, which the nurse thought was hilarious, and Barbara thought was outrageous), and attached to a blood pressure monitor. After one last kiss and squeeze of the hand from Barbara, I was rolled into surgery. I don't remember much after that except the white and stainless steel surrounding of the surgery room. A voice said, "Mr. Arbuckle would you start counting backwards from 100?" "Ok," I replied, "Well let's see, 100, 99, 98, 97, 96, 90…"

My next recollection is opening my eyes to Barbara's smile. I was told that things had gone smoothly, and that I was doing fine. I don't remember anything more until awakening in the room with Barbara, Royletta, Marseille, Jr., Jamillah, Andrea, and Beverly all looking at me with these funny looking half smiles on their faces. I didn't feel any pain, but I was thirsty. It was great being pampered and catered to. They fluffed up my pillows, gave me water and ice chips, adjusted the bed level and fussed over me for the rest of the evening. The nurses finally ran everyone off accept Barbara who remained with me for the rest of the night. In the middle of the night a team of doctors and nurses gathered around my bedside. Apparently while I slept, my blood pressure had elevated to a level of concern.

The doctors worked for the next three days to get control of my blood pressure. Pills and injections were the doctor's tools, Barbara and I used prayer. Typically prostate surgery is only a one night hospital stay. My time at Henry Ford Hospital extended to three nights and four days, as they worked to regain control of my blood pressure. Once the doctors were satisfied that my blood pressure had been stabilized, I was allowed to return home to begin recuperating and getting adjusted to life after a prostatectomy. That included learning how to maintain the catheter and other fun stuff like sitting on the little donut shaped cushion and taking the regiment of pills. Being required to wear the pads because I couldn't control the flow motivated me to do Keigel exercises as often as I could stand it, so I would only need the pads for as short a period of time as possible.

I was able to be up and about within a week. Dr. Walker had decided that I not return to work, during the three or four weeks between the two surgeries. He felt I should stay home and focus on total recuperation and preparing for the upcoming surgery which would be more invasive and taxing on my system. After a week at home, I would go to the marina each day and enjoy the peaceful and beautiful environment of the waterfront. I prayed and gave God thanks for what He had done, and was about to do. I took account of my life and the many blessings and miracles that had already occurred. I thanked God for the blessing of cancer and the healing power that He had placed in the minds and hands of the doctors. I thanked Him for the technological advances that had been made and for having health insurance and being in a financial position to have those things available to me.

Another miracle occurred during the time between surgeries. As I look back I know that this miracle is a testimony to the fact that cancer was truly a blessing, as difficult as that may be to grasp and accept. My sister Royletta from Gary, Indiana, my brothers Michael from Gary, Indiana and Montclair from Cincinnati, Ohio, and Montclair's daughter Aisha from Atlanta, Georgia, all came to have Thanksgiving dinner with me. We had never all been in the same room at the same time in all of our years of existence. This may not seem like a miracle to some, but rather just a normal occurrence to have dinner with your siblings, but as a result of being foster children, we had never, ever had the privilege of the pleasure. Had I not had cancer, or been blessed with cancer, we may have never made it happen. But because of the "Big C" there is a sense of urgency and things get done in short order. Thank you God! **Isaiah 60:1, Arise, shine, for thy light is come, and the glory of the Lord is risen upon thee.**

We had received the call from Dr. Lulek a week prior to the first surgery with the news that the health insurance company had approved and authorized the aneurysm repair surgery. We were so very thankful for having health insurance and having selected a HMO that would stand behind its' promise when it really mattered. The cost of the two procedures and associated costs for prescription medication, tests and follow-up care will exceed $100,000. We would be financially devastated if it were not for the health insurance. Thank you God for another miracle! **Psalm 63:5&7, My soul shall be satisfied as with marrow and fatness; and my mouth shall praise thee**

with joyful lips. Verse 7, Because thou hast been my help, therefore in the shadow of thy wings will I rejoice.

The days passed quickly and the tension mounted as time for the second surgery drew closer and closer. Dr. Walker prescribed Zoloft, an antidepressant, to help keep me calm although I felt I didn't need it. I prayed more and more and I was completely confident that God had another miracle in store for me. **Psalm 62:6, He only is my rock and my salvation: he is my defence; I shall not be moved.**

Chapter 31

December 5, 2007 arrived just as any other early winter day. It was cold but no snow had fallen yet. I was scheduled to arrive at the hospital at 7:30 a.m., so we were up and moving about the house early that morning. Barbara, her sister Beverly and my sister Royletta accompanied me to the hospital that morning. Marseille, Jr. had a class and would come to the hospital later in the day and wait with the others. I remember pressing the ladies to get me to the hospital on time. I joked that I didn't want to annoy any of the doctors that were supposed to work on me by being late and forcing them to work late. Actually I think I was at a point that I wanted it to be all over with.

As we walked into the waiting room and took our seats, I was once again surprised to see a member of the church ministerial staff walking into the room and looking about to find me. He came over to where we were sitting and greeted us all. He then sat down and we joined hands and prayed. It was very comforting and reassuring to have support from the church at a critical time. Shortly after our prayer ended my name was called out over the monitor and Barbara and I got up to make our way to the surgery prep area. As we were walking along the corridor I heard someone calling my name so I looked around to see my friend and Presiding Pastor of our church, Rev. C. Christian Adams.

It was very uplifting to see Christian striding toward me with his bright smile. He is a tall dark fellow that the ladies have always considered to be handsome. As usual he was fashionably decked out in a stylish suit and projected an essence of business professional demeanor. His handshake and embrace were warm and sincere. I had become rather chummy with Christian over the years. During my first stay in Detroit in the earlier 1980's, he and I had met on occasion socially through common acquaintances. When I returned in 1995 he was completing graduate work out East and then returned to work with his father at the church. He and I had developed a relationship over the last several years working together on various civic activities, mostly the Head Start program.

Christian told Barbara and me that he felt compelled to come by and share a word of prayer with us and offer the full support of his family and the church family. I thanked him as we walked toward the prep room. I ask the nurse if both Barbara and Christian could come with me and she said it would be ok for awhile. Barbara and Christian waited as I closed the curtain and put on the backless smock and sat on the side of the bed. They came in and we joined hands and prayed. After our prayer, Christian and I exchanged a few pleasantries about the weather and traffic, shortly after which he left. I truly felt uplifted by both visits and the prayers. As

I sat there holding Barbara's hand I felt ready to face any and everything.

The nurse came into the room and began to shave me and attach electrodes to monitor my heart rate and blood pressure. Next the anesthesiologist came into the room to tell me about the epidural needle that would be inserted into my spine. That would allow pain suppressing medication to be applied at the most affective point. He stressed the fact that controlling any pain that I might experience was one of his key objectives. I remember thinking to myself that sticking a needle into my spine doesn't seem like the right first step to eliminating pain. Later pain would become an ally; to experience pain is a confirmation that you are alive.

I don't remember much more about the actual surgery. Barbara told me that the procedure took over four hours. I have read the detailed report describing the operation and noticed that my blood pressure did elevate and cause some extra activity to take place in order to maintain control of it. My next clear recollection is Barbara calling my name and opening my eyes to see her smile. Although she was smiling she was batting her eyes to hold back tears. I'm not sure if they were tears of joy or pity. I wanted to speak but I couldn't. There was a tube in my mouth with tape around it and tubes in my nose. As I moved my head a bit left and right I could tell that there were tubes coming out of my neck. I rolled my eyes downward and saw there where tubes extending out of both arms and one in my left hand.

"Marsialle, you made it, you're ok!" Barbara's voice was shaken and just above a whisper. She leaned forward and kissed me on the forehead, although I couldn't feel her touch. I began opening my eyes wide and batting them as a signal that I understood what she was saying. "Mr. Arbuckle we're going to move you out of recovery into ICU," a voice said loudly. "We'll need to closely monitor your blood pressure and heart rate over the next 24 to 48 hours," said the same voice. Finally a face came into view that was attached to the loud voice. It was a woman in a nurse's uniform that I had not seen before. I would end up seeing lots of her over the next four days. The original 48 hours were extended to 72 hours and then 96 hours. My blood pressure and heart rate took a wild up and down ride during those hours.

The Intensive Care Unit is a unique world unto its own. Although the doctors told me that I was there to recover, it seemed that most of the people were there to die. It was the final battle ground for those facing the most extreme and severe illnesses. I was bedridden and couldn't move about so only the sounds around me would provide a clue as to what was occurring. Things would be silent and then suddenly the rushing about of feet and carts rolling through the corridor. I could hear voices of concern calling out instructions and making requests. Terminology that I had heard on medical television shows was drifting through the air.

I could hear the voice of family members consoling each other and asking questions. I heard the voice of a priest giving the last rites. I heard the voice of a minister reading or quoting Holy Scripture and performing the ceremony for the sacrament of Holy Communion. During the third night in ICU, I heard two families with such dramatically different emotions for the same situation, the death of a loved one. There was weeping, prayer, and consolation from one group. The other group let out shouts of anger and screamed demands at the medical staff. They shouted threats of medical malpractice law suits and physical violence toward the doctor. I could only think that the circumstances that were associated with the situation were very different, but ironically no matter what the circumstances the situation remained the same, someone had expired. No matter what the circumstances, or the reaction, the outcome of the situation did not change, someone was dead.

Each day Barbara would visit me during her lunch break and in the evening. The hospital would not allow her to stay the night in ICU with me. Since I could not speak for the first two days there wasn't much communication and not much need for her to be there. During the hours that passed I focused on being calm. If I could remain calm I thought; I would help lower my heart rate and blood pressure. The key to being calm was in believing that I was going to be ok. Believing that God was performing a miracle and that everything was going to be fine. It seemed appropriate to me that a vital element of my survival would be my ability to demonstrate my complete and total faith at a point when life or death was in the balance. I mentally repeated over and over; **Psalm 23, The Lord is my shepherd I shall not want. He maketh me to lie down in green pastures; he leadeth me beside the still waters. He restoreth my soul: he leadeth me in the paths of righteousness for his name's sake. Yea, though I walk through the valley of the shadow of death, I will fear no evil: for thou art with me; thy rod and thy staff they comfort me. Thou preparest a table before me in the presence of mine enemies: thou anointest my head with oil; my cup runneth over. Surely goodness** and mercy shall follow me all the days of my life: and I will dwell in the house of the Lord forever.

On day three the tube was removed from my mouth and throat. I told Barbara how happy I was to be alive and that I knew that God was going to allow me to make it. My blood pressure and heart rate continued to bounce around for another day and on day five it stabilized to a point that I was moved to a regular room. I remained hospitalized for several more days. They were difficult days filled with pain and medication. I continued my daily prayers and reciting of Psalm 23. I also thought often of a poem I learned during my time as a member of the Lampados Club while pledging Omega Psi Phi. Invictus by William Ernest Henley;

> Out of the night that covers me,
> Black as a Pit from pole to pole,
> I thank whatever gods may be
> For my unconquerable soul.
> In the fell clutch of circumstance
> I have not winced nor cried aloud.
> Under the bludgeoning of chance
> My head is bloody, but unbowed.
>
> Beyond this place of wrath and tears
> Looms but the Horror of the shade,
> And yet the menace of the years
> Finds, and shall find, me unafraid.
>
> It matters not how strait the gate,
> How charged with punishment the scroll,

I am the master of my fate:
I am the captain of my soul.

I have been finally allowed to return home. Recovery is slow and extremely painful. I've become too familiar with Morphine, Ibuprofen, Tylenol, Fentanyl, and other prescription pain control medications. I also have complications with my digestive system, which makes each trip to the restroom an adventure. I've lost forty five more pounds, making for a total of 85 pounds dropped since the heart attack. Things aren't perfect but I'm here. **Psalm 104:1, Bless the Lord, O my soul, O Lord my God, thou art very great; thou art clothed with honour and majesty.**

January 25, 2008 is my 50th birthday. Barbara has decided to give me a big birthday bash and invite lots of folk to celebrate the day with me. I'm so happy to be alive and enjoy a 50th birthday. I plan to return to work at Ford Motor Company in April of 2008 if possible and I'm capable. That will be an entirely new set of challenges. Our country is in the midst of the most intense economic downturn since the Great Depression. Mortgages are being foreclosed at an unprecedented rate in America. Bankruptcy and credit default are now commonplace. Companies are eliminating positions by the thousands, closing their doors and reneging on pension plans. Ford Motor Company has followed the downsizing trend and had three massive cutbacks amongst the salaried ranks. If the job at Ford goes away it could have a devastating impact on our lives. I won't let that worry me though, I've always believed that the man made the job and the job didn't make the man. I'm looking forward to meeting the challenge head on, because when I find myself in a crisis situation, a miracle is about to happen.

Just as I found that the cancer was a blessing, I may discover that the entire journey through illness may be a blessing. The event made me change my priorities. Things that at one time would have gotten me overly excited now have a different perspective. When life itself can no longer be taken for granted, things like a job or finances become secondary. I certainly will be able to deal with my employment situation with a higher degree of patience and confidence than I would have, had I not experienced the tribulations with my health. I know that God has a plan for me and that He has more for me to do.

I've taken the opportunity to do lots of reading during my time recovering and one of the books that I found to be very insightful and inspiring is "The Purpose Driven Life" by Rick Warren. I agree with the Wall Street Journal assessment that Warren's message is unassailable. I concur with his premise that true purpose in life is not found in self-absorption but through faith in action. Loving God through worship; showing love to my wife Barbara, my family, and others through service and ministry; sharing God's Word and message through evangelism; building and sharing in the body of Christ through fellowship; and developing into a true Christ-like being through discipleship are my top priorities.

It is my sincere hope that in recording some of the miracles that God has performed in my life, I will inspire and encourage someone to persevere and press on through the difficult journeys that life will lead you through. Yes, I proclaim the entire series of events in my life as miraculous;

- Being discovered by a social worker when abandoned by my biological parents.
- Being placed in a loving home with Christian parents.
- Having positive role models and mentors during my youth.
- Having the privilege to attend a Big Ten University on scholarship and joining an international fraternity with no financial means.
- Having my resume land on the desk of a fraternity brother, resulting in being hired by a multibillion dollar international corporation.
- Having the privilege of attending and completing graduate school with no financial means.
- Being relocated back to Indiana so I could care for my aging parents and provide love and support for other family members.
- Meeting, falling in love with and marrying the most beautiful and best lifelong partner I could ever have.
- Having beautiful children and grandchildren.
- Being relocated back to Michigan and re-directing my career at Ford Motor Company resulting in advancement and financial stability.
- Having the opportunity to serve the church and the community and providing positive opportunities and impact.
- Surviving both a car and motor cycle crash.
- Surviving a heart attack and getting control of my weight, heart rate and blood pressure.

- Surviving prostate cancer.
- Reuniting with my siblings.
- Surviving the abdominal aortic aneurysm and the surgery to repair it.

Yes they are all miraculous events directed by the hand of God. I thank God for His Saving Grace, Mercy, and Love. Throughout my writing you have noticed that I have infused the Holy Scriptures from the King James Version of The Holy Bible. I give praise and thanks to God that His Word has been manifested through my life. My desire in telling my story is to let my light shine that men may see God's great work and glorify God's name!

Psalm 105, O Give thanks unto the Lord; call upon his name: make known his deeds among the people. Sing unto him, sing psalms unto him: talk ye of all his wondrous works. Glory ye in his holy name: let the heart of them rejoice that seek the Lord. Yes I have a story to tell, my story is that I serve the one true and living God. I know that God lives; because He lives in me.

Until The Next Time...

Barbara & I at the Omega Fall Formal - Christmas 2009